Study Skills for Sixth Grade
Table of Contents

Study Skills for Sixth Grade
Introduction

Study Skills for Sixth Grade is designed to provide practice with and reinforcement of the thinking skills and strategies necessary for success at this grade level. It also reinforces the skills necessary for standardized achievement tests.

This book concentrates on the fundamentals of learning at this level. From following directions to the parts of a book, these are basics that all students need to know before they can move on to higher levels of thinking in these areas. This book is designed to give students the practice necessary to build strong foundations in understanding. Once these skills are mastered, students will be more likely to achieve success as they move forward.

Organization

This book is organized into five main areas for study: Following Directions, Using Reference Materials, Becoming Familiar with Story and Book Parts, Understanding Literature, and Strengthening Reading Comprehension. Each section focuses on important areas for skill reinforcement. There is a letter to send to parents which explains the purpose of the worksheets in this book.

The assessment can be given as a pre-test and post-test to evaluate improvement. On page 5 you will find a handy strategies chart which will help students stay focused on their work and keep the skills in perspective.

Use

This book is designed for independent use by students. Copies of the activities can be given to individuals, pairs of students, or small groups for completion. They can also be used as a center activity.

To begin, determine the implementation that fits your students' needs and your classroom structure. The following plan suggests a format for implementation.

1. **Explain** the purpose of these activities to the class. You may want to suggest that this work is meant for practice purposes and will not necessarily affect their grade. Discuss any questions students may have.

2. **Do** a practice activity together. Most sections have a page of explanation and practice that lends itself to guided practice. Go over the explanation with the students, let them try the practice activity, and then discuss the activity as a class.

3. **Assign** pages of the unit for independent or small-group study or for homework. The sections are designed so that no activity is more than two pages long. Many activities are one-page assignments.

4. **Determine** how you will monitor the assessment. Decide whether you want to

administer the assessment as a pre-test and post-test to keep in the students' portfolios, or if you want only to administer the test when the students complete the book. You may also wish to use the test to determine which students need reinforcement in certain areas and which students may already have mastered these skills.

Additional Notes

1. **Communication** Sign and send the Letter to Parents home with your students and encourage your students to share the letter with their parents. This will alert parents that their children may be bringing home papers for homework. It will encourage parents to become involved with the homework and help the child form good study habits. If the work is completed at school, decide if it will go into the students' portfolios for discussion at conference time.

2. **Student Communication** Be sure to discuss with your students what they will be doing and what it means. Assure the students that these worksheets are for practice purposes to help them improve their study skills. Make copies of the *Strategies for Success* to pass out to the students and post it on the wall for easy reference. As a class, talk about other strategies that could be included.

3. **Make It Fun** Make the work fun and meaningful when possible. For example, after a discussion and work with charts and graphs, find a way to relate the information to the students' own lives. If your class is doing a school project or there is a national event that has caught the interest of the class, take a survey and make a chart so that students can see their skills working in a real-life situation. Do a mixed-up play in which small groups get together independently and make up a plot, setting, and characters. When they get together, see how the pieces fit. They may have placed cowboys on a spaceship in a plot to rid the world of pollution forever!

Dear Parent:

Strong basic skills are important for all students. With study and practice of the basic skills, students have a much higher chance for achieving success as they move ahead through school.

We will be using *Study Skills for Sixth Grade* to work on and strengthen those skills necessary for success in the sixth grade. We will discuss the skills in class and then have pages for independent study. These pages may be completed in class, or they may be given as homework.

If your child brings work home, please consider the following suggestions:

- **Provide a quiet place to work.**
- **Go over the directions together.**
- **Encourage your child to do his or her best.**
- **Be available for questions should your child become confused or need some assistance. Remind your child to do just what the directions state.**
- **Check the lesson when it is complete. Note improvements as well as concerns.**

Help your child maintain a positive attitude about study skills. Let your child know that each lesson provides an opportunity to learn and grow. If your child expresses anxiety about these skills, help him or her understand what causes the stress. Talk about ways to deal with the anxiety.

Above all, enjoy this time you spend with your child. He or she will feel your support, and skills will improve with each activity completed.

Thank you for your help!

Cordially,

Study Skills for Sixth Grade
Strategies for Success

Purpose   Set a realistic goal. Develop a plan.

Planning   How much time do you have to achieve your goal?
                   Use your time well.

Prioritizing   Review what you need to do.
                   Decide what needs to be done first, second, and so on.

Persistence   Work toward your goal each day.
                   Don't give up.

Practice   In sports, crafts, music, or schoolwork, training is very important.
                   Keep at it.

Pacing   Study each day.
                   Don't wait until the last minute.

Study Skills 6, SV 8054-5

Name_____   Date_____

Read each question carefully. Fill in the answer circle or write the correct answer to each question.

1. Your name should be written at the top of this page. Ⓐ Underline your first name. Ⓑ Draw a circle around your last name. Ⓒ Write the date under your name. Ⓓ Do not do step B.

Use this chart to answer questions 2 and 3.

Average Time Spent on Homework by Jefferson Students Per Day

1995	2 hours
1996	1 hour, 45 minutes
1997	2 hours
1998	2 hours, 30 minutes

2. During which two years did students spend the same amount of time on homework?

_____

3. How much time did students spend on homework in 1998? _____

4. In what reference book would you look to find a synonym for *quickly*?
   Ⓐ dictionary   Ⓑ encyclopedia   Ⓒ thesaurus   Ⓓ atlas

5. Which of these parts of a book explains the meaning of special terms and can be found at the bottom of the page?
   Ⓐ glossary   Ⓑ footnotes   Ⓒ appendix   Ⓓ bibliography

6. Sean walked slowly back from the mailbox. "I can't believe it," he said. "They said my model would be here in two to four weeks, and it's been five weeks now."

   How does Sean feel?
   Ⓐ disappointed   Ⓑ frightened   Ⓒ cheerful   Ⓓ excited

7. John was at home sick, while his friends were at school making surprise get-well notes for him.

   Write the above sentence to change the point of view to first-person.

_____

Study Skills Grade 6, Assessment (p. 2)

8. In 1795 there were 453 post offices in the United States.
   What is the setting for the sentence above?
   Ⓐ inside the largest post office
   Ⓑ the post office in Washington
   Ⓒ the United States in 1795
   Ⓓ England in 1795

9. Was it possible? Would Mr. Samuels let a girl ride for the Pony Express? I could feel the excitement rise in my stomach, but I was confident I could do the job.

   Which choice best identifies the type of literature above?
   Ⓐ historical fiction   Ⓑ fantasy   Ⓒ realistic fiction

10. Read this sentence and choose the answer that has the same, or nearly the same, meaning as the sentence.

    The tree fought the wind with its branches.
    Ⓐ A battle was being fought beneath the tree.
    Ⓑ The tree branches were moving in the wind.

11. The leaves are a beautiful shade of red in the fall.
    Is the above statement a *fact* or an *opinion*? _____

12. Read this sentence. Circle the *cause* (why) and underline the *effect* (what).

    Kay didn't have a pencil since she loaned hers to me.

13. The Davis family was having a picnic down by the lakeshore. It was the last night in the cottage before returning home. Dark, threatening clouds were gathering in the west, and the wind was becoming gusty.

    What will the Davis family do next?

    _____

14. Read these facts and write a generalization using the facts.
    My father is a kindergarten teacher. My mother teaches chemistry.

    _____

15. Write whether each sentence is a *true statement*, a *valid opinion* (backed up with some facts), or an *invalid opinion*.
    Ⓐ Rain has been known to shrink people._____
    Ⓑ I think that dogs are the best pets._____
    Ⓒ In 1959, Hawaii became the fiftieth state. _____
    Ⓓ Many people think pigs are very clean. _____

● ●

Study Skills Grade 6, Assessment (p. 3)

16. The whale is often mistaken for a fish instead of a mammal. The whale breathes air, has hair on parts of its body, and is warm-blooded. Baby whales, called calves, get milk from their mother's body. These are all characteristics of mammals.

This story is mainly about _____.
Ⓐ baby whales called calves
Ⓑ whales being mammals
Ⓒ habits of the blue whale
Ⓓ the whale's blood

17. Jim's leg <u>fracture</u> caused him to be in a cast for six weeks.

What is the meaning of *fracture* in the sentence above?
Ⓐ twist   Ⓑ infection   Ⓒ break   Ⓓ mend

18. Thomas Edison was probably the world's greatest inventor. He invented the phonograph and motion pictures. His most famous invention is the electric light, and he also made many improvements on the telegraph, though he did not invent it. He would often nap in his lab and continue working upon waking, regardless of the time of day.

What was Thomas Edison's most famous invention? _____

19. Jay had to remember the food for the camping trip. He also wanted to take the camera. If he had time today, he would call his friend Jimmy about going to the movies next Saturday.

Number the events in the order of their importance to the camping trip.
_____ call Jimmy
_____ take food
_____ take the camera

20. Read the following statement and draw a line around the persuasive technique used by the writer.

Buy Sudsy Soap! It's the soap of the smartest shoppers.
Ⓐ bandwagon   Ⓑ glad words/sad words   Ⓒ plain folks   Ⓓ glittering generalities

21. Read the story. Then fill in the answer circle in front of the choice that best completes the sentence.

The car was loaded with luggage. We had left a note with the neighbor about feeding the cat each day for the next two weeks. We had talked to the paper girl about not leaving the paper. It was time to go!

It is most likely _____.
Ⓐ moving day   Ⓑ vacation time   Ⓒ a garage sale   Ⓓ time for a picnic

• •

TO THE LETTER

Everyone has made a mistake because he or she didn't follow directions. It just takes a minute, but we often begin working because we think we know what to do.

Written directions are often not followed correctly because the following rules are ignored:

1. Directions should always be read.
   Often people are sure they know what to do without reading the directions. Read the directions anyway just to be sure.

2. Read *all* of the directions before beginning.
   Sometimes the last part of the directions will change, in some way, what you were told to do in the first part.

3. Directions should be followed in the order they are given.
   Doing things out of order can change the result. Think about trying to make a cake by adding the eggs after it has been in the oven. It will not turn out right!

> **To Follow Directions:**
> **1. READ the directions carefully.**
> **2. READ all of the directions before beginning.**
> **3. FOLLOW the directions in the order they are given.**

DIRECTIONS:

Read these directions and follow them exactly.

1. Draw a circle in the space below.
   In the circle, print the word that is the color of the sky on a clear day.
   Draw a box around the circle.
   Write your first name in cursive under the box.

2. Make two dots in the space below.
   Connect the dots with a straight line.
   Print the word "HELLO" above the line you have drawn.

Go on to the next page.

TO THE LETTER (P. 2)

DIRECTIONS:

Read the steps below.

> **Remember, To Follow Directions:**
> 1. READ the directions carefully.
> 2. READ all of the directions before beginning.
> 3. FOLLOW the directions in the order they are given.

DIRECTIONS:

Read the following directions, think about them, and answer the questions.

1. Print your first name, middle initial, and last name in the upper right-hand corner of the paper.
2. Print your teacher's last name under your name.
3. Print your room number under the teacher's name.
4. Skip a line and number from 1 to 10.
5. List, next to the numbers, your ten favorite foods.
6. Do not do #3.

1. What should you do just before numbering from 1 to 10?
   - Ⓐ Skip a line.
   - Ⓑ List foods.
   - Ⓒ Write your name.
   - Ⓓ Print your name.

2. What step should you not do?
   - Ⓐ #1
   - Ⓑ #2
   - Ⓒ #3
   - Ⓓ #4

3. Where should you put your teacher's name?
   - Ⓐ upper left-hand corner, under your name
   - Ⓑ upper right-hand corner, under your name
   - Ⓒ not at all
   - Ⓓ next to the number 10

4. Where do you write your ten favorite foods?
   - Ⓐ beside your teacher's name
   - Ⓑ under your room number
   - Ⓒ next to the numbers 1 to 10
   - Ⓓ beside number 3

Following Directions

• •

THE WAY TO SAY IT

 **DIRECTIONS:**

Read the steps below.

> **Remember, To Pronounce New Words:**
> 1. FIND the entry word in the dictionary.
> 2. LOOK at the way it is divided into syllables.
> 3. FIND the phonetic respelling.
> 4. USE the pronunciation key.
> 5. DECIDE which syllable is spoken most strongly.
> 6. SAY the new word.

Now, think about the pronunciation of each word. Then draw a line around the correct answer.

hy•giene [hī´ jēn´]

1. The last syllable in *hygiene* sounds like:
gin   Jean   Jane

pneu•mo•nia [n(y)o͞o•mōn´ yə]

2. The first syllable in *pneumonia* begins with the same sound as:
pony   full   notice

che•nille [shə•nēl´]

3. The last syllable in the word *chenille* rhymes with:
Nell   nil   kneel

4. The first syllable in *chenille* begins with the same sound as:
carpet   chair   shine

gus•set [gus´ it]

5. The second syllable of *gusset* rhymes with:
pet   pit   put

a	add	i	it	o͝o	took	oi	oil
ā	ace	ī	ice	o͞o	pool	ou	pout
â	care	o	odd	u	up	ng	ring
ä	palm	ō	open	û	burn	th	thin
e	end	ô	order	yo͞o	fuse	th	this
ē	equal					zh	vision

ə = { a in *above*   e in *sicken*   i in *possible*
       o in *melon*   u in *circus* }

HBJ School Dictionary

6. The syllable spoken most strongly in *gusset* is the:
first   second

Go on to the next page.

Pronunciation

THE WAY TO SAY IT (P. 2)

DIRECTIONS:

Think about the pronunciation of each word. Then draw a line around the correct answer.

Seoul [sōl]

7. The word *Seoul* rhymes with:

roll   reel   rule

chic [shēk]

8. The first sound in *chic* is the same as in the word:

chin   kid   she

Re•noir [ren´ wär]

9. The first syllable in the name *Renoir* rhymes with:

keen   pen   see

10. The syllable spoken most strongly in *Renoir* is the:

first   second

drach•ma [drak´ mə]

11. The first syllable in *drachma* rhymes with:

rock   rake   rack

par•fait [pär•fā´]

12. The first syllable of *parfait* rhymes with:

car   dare   fur

a	add	i	it	o͝o	took	oi	oil
ā	ace	ī	ice	o͞o	pool	ou	pout
â	care	o	odd	u	up	ng	ring
ä	palm	ō	open	û	burn	th	thin
e	end	ô	order	yo͞o	fuse	th	this
ē	equal					zh	vision

ə = { a in *above*   e in *sicken*   i in *possible*
      o in *melon*   u in *circus* }

HBJ School Dictionary

13. The syllable spoken most strongly in *parfait* is the:

first   second

14. The second syllable of *parfait* sounds like:

fight   fate   Fay

co•quette [kō•ket´]

15. The second syllable of *coquette* starts with the same sound as:

cut   quiet   check

ci•ca•da [si•kā´ də]

16. The second syllable of *cicada* rhymes with:

day   ma   sad

Pronunciation

• •

LOOK IT UP

 **DIRECTIONS:**

Read the following dictionary entry carefully.

raccoon *n.* [Am. Ind. arakunem, scratcher] a small nocturnal mammal of N. America.

The words inside the brackets tell the history of the word, including the language that is its source. Some words come from other words, and some words we use every day have been taken from other languages.

In the entry above, you are told that the word *raccoon* comes from the American Indian word *arakunem,* which means scratcher. It is easy to see why this name is a good one for this animal, which is an expert scratcher.

Many times the language source is abbreviated. Here are some common abbreviations:

Am. - American	Du. - Dutch
Am. Ind. - American Indian	Eng. - English
Am. Sp. - American Spanish	G. - German
Brit. - British	Gr. - Greek
L. - Latin	

It is not necessary to memorize them. They will be in your dictionary, usually right before the first entry word.

> **To Determine Word Origins and Histories:**
> 1. READ the dictionary entry carefully.
> 2. LOOK for information about the word's history.
> 3. LOOK for information about the origin of the word.
> 4. THINK about how the word we use came to be.

Now, look at the dictionary entry and answer the questions.

gram *n.* [Gr. gramma, small weight] the basic unit of weight in the metric system.

1. From what language did the word *gram* originate?

_____

2. What was the original word?

_____

Go on to the next page.

Name_____ Date_____

LOOK IT UP (P. 2)

 **DIRECTIONS:**

Read the steps below.

> **To Determine Word Origins and Histories:**
> 1. READ the dictionary entry carefully.
> 2. LOOK for information about the word's history.
> 3. LOOK for information about the origin of the word.
> 4. THINK about how the word we use came to be.

Look at each dictionary entry and answer the questions.

noose *n.* [L. nodus, a knot] a loop formed in a rope by means of a slipknot.

3. From what language did the word *noose* originate?

_____

4. What was the original word?

_____

5. What was the meaning of the original word?

_____

car *n.* [L. carrus, chariot] any vehicle on wheels.

6. From what language did the word *car* originate?

_____

7. What was the original word?

_____

8. What was the meaning of the original word?

_____

skunk *n.* [Am. Ind.] a small bushy-tailed mammal having black fur with white stripes down the back.

9. From what language did the word *skunk* originate?

_____

Study Skills 6, SV 8054-5

Name _____   Date _____

● ●

JEFFERSON SCHOOL

Sometimes it is useful to compare the information on charts, graphs, tables, and lists. It sometimes happens that comparing two sources of information can give a much clearer picture than either one of them alone. Let's look at an example.

*Average 24-Hour Schedule
for Gary S. in 1998*

Sleep	x x x x x x x x
School	x x x x x x x
Homework	x x x
TV/Play	x x
Other	x x x x

x = 1 hour

*Average Time Spent
on Homework by Jefferson
Students Per Day*

1995	2 hours
1996	1 hour, 45 minutes
1997	2 hours
1998	2 hours, 30 minutes

Let's compare the graph and the chart. Gary S. spent 3 hours a day on homework in 1998, according to the graph on the left. Meanwhile, the average student in Gary's school only spent 2 hours, 30 minutes a day on homework, according to the chart on the right. This means that Gary is spending more time than the average Jefferson Elementary student. That information might be important for Gary, his parents, or his teachers to know. We got that information by comparing the two information sources.

To Compare the Information on Charts, Graphs, Tables, and Lists:
1. **LOOK** at each information source carefully.
2. **DECIDE** what information each one is giving you.
3. **COMPARE** the information, and see if you can make a connection between the two that tells you more than you knew before.

DIRECTIONS: Compare these two information sources and answer the questions.

*Favorite Hobbies of
Jefferson Students 1997*
1. Listening to music
2. Baseball/softball
3. Reading
4. Skateboarding
5. Shopping
6. Roller skating

*Favorite Hobbies of
Jefferson Students 1998*
1. Listening to music
2. Watching television
3. Skateboarding
4. Baseball/softball
5. Shopping
6. Roller skating

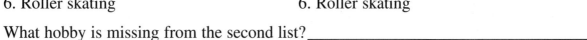

1. What hobby is missing from the second list?_____

2. Who might be concerned about the missing item?_____

Go on to the next page.

JEFFERSON SCHOOL (P. 2)

DIRECTIONS:

Read the steps below.

> **Remember, To Compare the Information on Charts, Graphs, Tables, and Lists:**
> 1. **LOOK** at each information source carefully.
> 2. **DECIDE** what information each one is giving you.
> 3. **COMPARE** the information, and see if you can make a connection between the two that tells you more than you knew before.

Compare the two information sources. Fill in the answer circle in front of the correct answer.

Bags of Peanuts sold by Jefferson students

Grade	Peanuts sold
K	81
1	77
2	60
3	45
4	62
5	87
6	102

Top 5 Salespersons

Name	Grade	Bags of Peanuts sold
Jerry S.	6	82
Mary D.	4	25
Jeff O.	1	22
Julia B.	6	12
Sue K.	2	10

3. Which grade sold the most peanuts?
  Ⓐ kindergarten   Ⓑ fifth   Ⓒ fourth   Ⓓ sixth

4. Compare the two tables. What information do you now have about the sixth-grade sales?
  Ⓐ The second grade sold the most peanuts in the sale.
  Ⓑ No sixth-grader sold many peanuts for the sale.
  Ⓒ Girls are not good at selling peanuts.
  Ⓓ Two people in the sixth grade did most of the work.

5. Which grade sold the least number of peanuts?
  Ⓐ kindergarten   Ⓑ first   Ⓒ third   Ⓓ fifth

6. Who were the two top salespersons?
  Ⓐ Mary and Jeff   Ⓑ Jerry and Mary
  Ⓒ Sue and Jerry   Ⓓ Julia and Jerry

Name _____   Date _____

AMERICANA

 **DIRECTIONS:**

Look at the chart. Fill in the answer circle in front of the correct answer.

AMERICAN STATESMEN		
Name	**Dates**	**Accomplishments**
Benjamin Franklin American Patriot	1706-1790	Worked for American independence
George Washington U.S. President	1732-1799	Led colonies in fight for independence
Thomas Jefferson U.S. President	1743-1826	Wrote the *Declaration of Independence*
James Madison U.S. President	1751-1836	Helped write the U.S. *Constitution*
James Monroe U.S. President	1758-1831	Issued the *Monroe Doctrine*
Henry Clay U.S. Senator	1777-1852	Worked for peaceful end to slavery problem
John Calhoun U.S. Vice-President	1782-1850	Opposed a strong federal government
Daniel Webster U.S. Senator	1782-1852	Helped avoid civil war for 30 years

1. What two statesmen died the same year?
   - Ⓐ Clay and Webster
   - Ⓑ Calhoun and Webster
   - Ⓒ Washington and Jefferson
   - Ⓓ Madison and Jefferson

2. What two statesmen were U.S. Presidents?
   - Ⓐ Franklin and Washington
   - Ⓑ Jefferson and Monroe
   - Ⓒ Calhoun and Webster
   - Ⓓ Franklin and Calhoun

3. Which statesman worked to end slavery?
   - Ⓐ Thomas Jefferson
   - Ⓑ Daniel Webster
   - Ⓒ George Washington
   - Ⓓ Henry Clay

Go on to the next page.

Name_____   Date_____

AMERICANA (P. 2)

 **DIRECTIONS:**

Compare the lists. Fill in the answer circle in front of the correct answer.

ENGLISH WORDS		
American English		**British English**
subway	=	tube
french fries	=	chips
potato chips	=	crisps
garbage can	=	dust bin
washcloth	=	face flannel
dessert	=	sweet
checkers	=	draughts
thumbtacks	=	drawing pins
freight train	=	goods train
gasoline	=	petrol
rent	=	let
scratch pad	=	scribbling block
sidewalk	=	pavement
public school	=	council school
underpass	=	subway
policemen	=	bobbies
apartment	=	flat

4. What is the British word for the American word *checkers*?
Ⓐ petrol   Ⓑ draughts   Ⓒ drawing pins   Ⓓ sweets

5. What is the American word for the British term *face flannel*?
Ⓐ thumbtacks   Ⓑ garbage can   Ⓒ policeman   Ⓓ washcloth

6. What is a British word for *gasoline*?
Ⓐ petrol   Ⓑ gasoline   Ⓒ draughts   Ⓓ flat

7. The British let a flat; Americans _____.
Ⓐ take a subway   Ⓑ rent an apartment
Ⓒ use a washcloth   Ⓓ use the sidewalk

Name_____   Date_____

TO THE LIBRARY

What are some sources of information in the library?

Book Catalogs

At one time, most libraries had a card catalog. This was a set of drawers, each with hundreds of small cards in them. The drawers were arranged in alphabetical order, and each drawer had its proper label. To find a book, you had to flip through the little cards, until you reached the right one. Searching for a book this way could take a long time.

Now, most libraries have a book catalog on computer. To find a book, you search for it using three categories: title, author, or subject. Now the search takes only seconds.

On the library shelves, fiction books are arranged alphabetically by the author's last name. Nonfiction books are arranged by subject. Each nonfiction book has a special number on it that reveals its subject. This number also appears on the book's computer entry to allow you to find the book more easily.

Reference Materials

1. Magazines and newspapers (periodicals) have recent events, articles, advertisements, editorials, and entertainment information.
2. Telephone directories have names, addresses, and phone numbers.
3. Encyclopedias have general information.
4. The thesaurus has synonyms and antonyms.
5. The dictionary has meanings, spellings, and histories of words.
6. An almanac has facts, figures, and statistics – updated each year.

> **To Use a Book Catalog and Reference Materials:**
> 1. **THINK** about the kind of information you need.
> 2. **DECIDE** whether that information would be in the book catalog, in some reference material, or elsewhere.
> 3. **USE** the information source you selected to find the information you need.

DIRECTIONS:

Fill in the blanks below.

1. I am interested in books about the American Revolution.

   I would search using _____.

2. I want to know a synonym for *coagulate*. I would look in a(n) _____.

Go on to the next page.

Periodicals, Book Catalogs, and Reference Works

Name_____ Date_____

TO THE LIBRARY (P. 2)

 **DIRECTIONS:**

Read the steps below.

> **Remember, To Use a Book Catalog and Reference Materials:**
> 1. **THINK about the kind of information you need.**
> 2. **DECIDE whether that information would be in the book catalog, in some reference material, or elsewhere.**
> 3. **USE the information source you selected to find the information you need.**

Fill in each blank with *author, title,* or *subject.*

3. I would like to read more books by Stella Pevsner. I would search using

the _____.

4. I want to read the book *Tales of a Fourth Grade Nothing.* I would search using

_____.

5. I want to know more about whales. I would search using _____.

Fill in the blank with the correct reference material.

6. I want to know all about dinosaurs. I would look in the _____.

7. I need to know the meaning of the word *orthodox.* I would look in the _____.

8. I want the phone number for Flaky Pizza. I would look in the _____.

9. I want to read about the fire that happened downtown today. I would look

in the _____.

10. I want to find the world population statistics for last year. I would look in

the _____.

• •

SELECT THE SOURCE

Read the steps below.

> **To Identify the Appropriate Source Used to Obtain Information:**
> 1. **THINK** about the information you need.
> 2. **DECIDE** if the information can be found in a dictionary, encyclopedia, atlas, newspaper, or telephone directory.

Read the sentence. Fill in the answer circle in front of the correct answer.

1. To find the main highways in the state of Texas, you would look in the _____.
  Ⓐ dictionary   Ⓑ newspaper
  Ⓒ atlas   Ⓓ telephone directory

2. To find the meaning of the word *extemporaneous,* you would look in the _____.
  Ⓐ dictionary   Ⓑ encyclopedia
  Ⓒ telephone directory   Ⓓ atlas

3. To find the weather forecast for tomorrow, you would look in the _____.
  Ⓐ telephone directory   Ⓑ dictionary
  Ⓒ newspaper   Ⓓ encyclopedia

4. To find information for a report about Thomas Edison, you would look in the _____.
  Ⓐ encyclopedia   Ⓑ dictionary
  Ⓒ atlas   Ⓓ newspaper

5. To find the address for the Jiffy Printing Company, you would look in the _____.
  Ⓐ encyclopedia   Ⓑ dictionary
  Ⓒ atlas   Ⓓ telephone directory

Go on to the next page.

Name _____   Date _____

SELECT THE SOURCE (P. 2)

DIRECTIONS:

Read the sentence. Fill in the answer circle in front of the correct answer.

6. To find the telephone number to call for Brighton Elementary School, you would look in the _____.
Ⓐ dictionary
Ⓑ telephone directory
Ⓒ encyclopedia
Ⓓ newspaper

7. To find the way to pronounce the word *melee*, you would look in the _____.
Ⓐ encyclopedia
Ⓑ dictionary
Ⓒ newspaper
Ⓓ atlas

8. To find how far it is between Dallas and Houston, you would look in the _____.
Ⓐ atlas
Ⓑ dictionary
Ⓒ encyclopedia
Ⓓ newspaper

9. To find the history of the word *coyote,* you would look in the _____.
Ⓐ newspaper
Ⓑ atlas
Ⓒ telephone directory
Ⓓ dictionary

10. To find information about the Treaty of Ghent, you would look in the _____.
Ⓐ newspaper
Ⓑ telephone directory
Ⓒ dictionary
Ⓓ encyclopedia

FOOTNOTES AND APPENDICES

You are probably familiar with many of the parts of a book. Here are a few you probably use all of the time:

Table of Contents   Preface
Title page   Copyright page
Index   Bibliography

There are two parts that might be new to you, footnotes and the appendix.

Footnotes are notes at the bottom of the page. A small number next to a word or phrase in the reading tells you to look at the bottom of the page for a matching number. There you will be given additional information. It might be (1) an explanation of the meaning of special terms, or (2) the source of facts, ideas, or quotations.

The appendix is a section at the end of the book where an author gives additional information to help the reader understand the material in the book. The appendix is usually found in a nonfiction book and might contain charts, maps, graphs, tables, or other material.

To use Footnotes and the Appendix:
1. READ the material carefully.
2. NOTICE if footnotes are used, and, if so, take advantage of the helpful information.
3. CHECK to see if there is an appendix in the back that might also have helpful information.

DIRECTIONS:

Write *footnote* or *appendix* next to each description.

1. bottom of page _____

2. graph or map _____

3. end of book _____

4. gives a meaning _____

5. gives a source _____

6. table or chart _____

Go on to the next page.

FOOTNOTES AND APPENDICES (P. 2)

 **DIRECTIONS:**

Read the steps below.

> **Remember, To Use Footnotes and the Appendix:**
> 1. **READ the material carefully.**
> 2. **NOTICE if footnotes are used, and, if so, take advantage of the helpful information.**
> 3. **CHECK to see if there is an appendix in the back that might also have helpful information.**

Fill in the answer circle in front of the choice that best answers the question.

7. Where could I find the name of the author of the book?
- Ⓐ footnote
- Ⓑ appendix
- Ⓒ elsewhere

8. Where could I find a list of chess clubs in a book about championship chess?
- Ⓐ footnote
- Ⓑ appendix
- Ⓒ elsewhere

9. Where could I find the source of a quote on a page?
- Ⓐ footnote
- Ⓑ appendix
- Ⓒ elsewhere

10. Where could I find the date the book was published?
- Ⓐ footnote
- Ⓑ appendix
- Ⓒ elsewhere

11. Where could I find a map of the sites of Civil War memorials in a book about the Civil War?
- Ⓐ footnote
- Ⓑ appendix
- Ⓒ elsewhere

KNOW WHERE TO LOOK

 **DIRECTIONS:**

Read the steps below.

> **To Use the Parts of a Book to Obtain Information:**
> 1. **THINK about the information you need.**
> 2. **DECIDE if the information can be found in the preface, copyright page, table of contents, glossary, or index.**
> 3. **LOOK for the information.**

Read the sentence. Fill in the answer circle in front of the correct answer.

1. To find the meaning for the word *conservation* used in a science book you are reading, you would look in the _____.
  Ⓐ index
  Ⓑ glossary
  Ⓒ table of contents
  Ⓓ copyright page

2. To find the page number for the beginning of Chapter 5, you would look in the _____.
  Ⓐ index
  Ⓑ preface
  Ⓒ table of contents
  Ⓓ glossary

3. To find the date the book you are reading was published, you would look in the _____.
  Ⓐ copyright page
  Ⓑ table of contents
  Ⓒ glossary
  Ⓓ preface

4. To find out why the book was written, you would look in the _____.
  Ⓐ table of contents
  Ⓑ index
  Ⓒ copyright page
  Ⓓ preface

Go on to the next page.

• •

KNOW WHERE TO LOOK (P. 2)

DIRECTIONS:

Read the sentence. Fill in the answer circle in front of the correct answer.

5. To find the publishing company of the book you are reading, you would look in the _____.
- Ⓐ copyright page
- Ⓑ table of contents
- Ⓒ preface
- Ⓓ index

6. To find all the pages in the book where you would find information about George Washington, you would look in the _____.
- Ⓐ glossary
- Ⓑ index
- Ⓒ table of contents
- Ⓓ preface

7. To find how to pronounce a word in the social studies book you are reading, you would look in the _____.
- Ⓐ index
- Ⓑ table of contents
- Ⓒ copyright page
- Ⓓ glossary

8. To find the beginning page number of a certain story you want to read in your reading book, you would look in the _____.
- Ⓐ index
- Ⓑ glossary
- Ⓒ preface
- Ⓓ table of contents

Name _____   Date _____

• •

PUT YOURSELF IN THEIR SHOES

 **DIRECTIONS:**

Read the following sentences and decide how the character feels.

Susan ran into the room and slid to a stop. There was a big grin on her face, and she held up her spelling paper.

You probably decided that Susan was excited and happy about her spelling paper. Your clues were her running in and the grin on her face.

There are three ways to decide how a character is feeling.

Actions
The character's actions tell you a lot. How does the character move? What is the expression on the character's face?

Dialogue
If the character is involved in a conversation, there are often clues to the character's feelings.

Character's Own Words
The character can say something that explains his or her feelings.

After you explain how a character is feeling, take the time to understand those feelings. It can help you to understand the story. Sometimes it can even help you to understand yourself better.

> **To Understand the Feelings of Characters:**
> 1. **READ** their story carefully.
> 2. **LOOK** for clues about how the characters are feeling.
> 3. **THINK** about those feelings to gain an understanding of the characters.

Now read each story below and decide how the character is feeling.

1. Sal stood with his hands made into fists at his side. There was a determined look on his face as he shouted at Lenny, "You are a bully, and I don't like it!"

_____

2. The little girl hid behind her mother and occasionally peeked out at her mother's friend.

_____

Go on to the next page.

Character

Study Skills 6, SV 8054-5

• •

PUT YOURSELF IN THEIR SHOES (P. 2)

DIRECTIONS:

Read the steps below.

> **Remember, To Understand the Feelings of Characters:**
> 1. **READ their story carefully.**
> 2. **LOOK for clues about how the characters are feeling.**
> 3. **THINK about those feelings to gain an understanding of the characters.**

Read each selection. Fill in the answer circle in front of the choice that best answers the question.

   Lacey came in from school and threw down her books. Homework could wait. She ran into the backyard and called for her new puppy. When Lacey knelt down to hug him, he gave her sloppy kisses in return.

3. How does Lacey feel?
   Ⓐ scared   Ⓑ disappointed   Ⓒ angry   Ⓓ excited

4. Why does Lacey feel that way?
   Ⓐ Her puppy seems to be sick.
   Ⓑ Lacey has to do homework.
   Ⓒ Lacey has a new puppy.
   Ⓓ School is out for the year.

   Sean walked slowly back from the mailbox. "I can't believe it," he said. "They said my model would be here in two to four weeks, and it's been five weeks now."

5. How does Sean feel?
   Ⓐ disappointed   Ⓑ cheerful   Ⓒ frightened   Ⓓ excited

6. Why does he feel that way?
   Ⓐ He couldn't mail his letter today.
   Ⓑ His model had arrived broken.
   Ⓒ Sean has lost his mom's mail.
   Ⓓ He is tired of waiting.

Character

Name_____   Date_____

POINT OF VIEW

What is the difference between these two sentences?

   I studied for three hours last night.
   Gary studied for three hours last night.

In the first sentence, the person is speaking for himself. In the second sentence, someone is telling about Gary. This is the point of view of each sentence. *Point of view* simply means who is telling the story.

In the first-person point of view, the action in a story is described from the point of view of one of the characters. The character will use the pronouns *I, me, my,* and *myself.*

In the third-person point of view, the story is told by a narrator (storyteller) who is not a character in the story. The narrator will use the pronouns *she, her, he, his, they,* and *their.*

There are two kinds of third-person point of view.

Limited third-person
In this kind of third-person point of view, the narrator tells the story through one character. Only the thoughts, feelings, and actions of that character will be told.

Omniscient
This word means "all-knowing." In this kind of story, the narrator will know *everything.* The past and future are known. Things happening away from the characters are known. Usually, the reader knows more than any of the characters.

To Recognize First- and Third-Person Points of View:
1. **READ the story carefully.**
2. **LOOK for the use of the clue pronouns.**
3. **DECIDE if the point of view is first- or third-person.**
4. **DECIDE (in third-person only) if the point of view is limited or omniscient.**

   Change these sentences from first-person to third-person point of view.

1. I wore my new shoes to school yesterday.

_____

2. I drove the truck by myself until my father made me stop.

_____

Point of View
Study Skills 6, SV 8054-5

Name _____ Date _____

THE TRUE VIEW

 **DIRECTIONS:**

Read the steps below.

> **Remember, To Recognize First- and Third-Person Points of View:**
> 1. READ the story carefully.
> 2. LOOK for the use of the clue pronouns.
> 3. DECIDE if the point of view is first- or third-person.
> 4. DECIDE (in third-person only) if the point of view is limited or omniscient.

Now, read each sentence. Fill in the answer circle in front of the choice that best tells the point of view.

1. The dog had no way of knowing that its owner was nearby.
   Ⓐ first-person
   Ⓑ limited third-person
   Ⓒ omniscient third-person

2. My favorite movie was playing at the theater.
   Ⓐ first-person
   Ⓑ limited third-person
   Ⓒ omniscient third-person

3. John was at home sick, while his friends were at school making surprise get-well notes for him.
   Ⓐ first-person
   Ⓑ limited third-person
   Ⓒ omniscient third-person

4. Sally walked down the street watching herself in store windows.
   Ⓐ first-person
   Ⓑ limited third-person
   Ⓒ omniscient third-person

5. If he had known they were coming, he would have been ready.
   Ⓐ first-person
   Ⓑ limited third-person
   Ⓒ omniscient third-person

A TIME AND A PLACE

The *setting* of a story is the *time* and *place* where story events occur.

What is the setting of this sentence?

As the boy and his grandfather neared the summit of the mountain, the sun broke through the clouds.

The setting in this sentence is the summit (top) of a mountain.

Now, what is the setting in this sentence?

The summer sun beat down mercilessly on the workers in the field.

This might seem harder, but it really isn't! The setting can also be the time when a story event happens. In this second sentence, the setting is in the summer and in a field.

> **To Describe the Setting of a Story:**
> 1. **READ** the story carefully.
> 2. **DECIDE** where it is taking place.
> 3. **DECIDE** when it is taking place.

Now, read each story and decide on its setting (time and place).

On the 30th of May, 1922, the Lincoln Memorial in Washington, D.C., was dedicated and opened to the public. Inside, there is a large statue of Lincoln carved by the American sculptor Daniel Chester French.

1. time_____

2. place_____

Last fall, our football team won all of its games. Our small town really backed the team and sent a busload of fans to every game.

3. time_____

4. place_____

Name_____ Date_____

SETTING IT UP

Read the steps below.

> **Remember, To Describe the Setting of a Story:**
> 1. READ the story carefully.
> 2. DECIDE where it is taking place.
> 3. DECIDE when it is taking place.

Read each selection. Fill in the answer circle in front of the choice that best answers each question.

Every spring, my dad works at the regional track meet at the local high school. He works as the timer and helps with cleanup. I like to go with him and watch the pole-vaulters. That's what I want to do when I get old enough.

1. What is the setting for this story?
- Ⓐ a park with a running track
- Ⓑ the high-school track meet
- Ⓒ a school for pole-vaulters
- Ⓓ spring training for baseball

2. What time of year does this story take place?
- Ⓐ fall
- Ⓑ winter
- Ⓒ spring
- Ⓓ summer

Sometimes at night, I sit in my room and think about my grandfather. I don't really feel sad. I just think of the things we did together and how he listened to my problems. Even when I was little, he took me seriously and made me feel important. I miss him.

3. What is the setting for this story?
- Ⓐ Grandfather's room downstairs
- Ⓑ after school in my room
- Ⓒ at night in the kitchen
- Ⓓ at night in my own room

In 1795, there were 453 post offices in the United States.

4. What is the setting for this sentence?
- Ⓐ inside the largest post office
- Ⓑ the post office in Washington
- Ⓒ 1795 in Great Britain
- Ⓓ the United States in 1795

Setting

Study Skills 6, SV 8054-5

• •

NONFICTION OR FICTION?

Nonfiction is based on facts.
Fiction is literature that has parts that are not true.

Here are some types of nonfiction: autobiography, biography, interview, and journal/diary.

Here are some types of fiction:

Historical fiction
There are two kinds of historical fiction. One kind will have real characters from the past, but they will do things and have conversations that are made up. The other kind of historical fiction involves real events, but has made-up characters.

Realistic fiction
This kind of fiction sounds as though it could really happen, but it is all made up.

Fantasy
Nothing is impossible in fantasy. Fairy tales, myths, legends, and science fiction are all fantasy stories.

> **To Respond to Forms of Literature:**
> 1. **READ** the selection carefully.
> 2. **THINK** about the people and places in the selection.
> 3. **DECIDE** if the selection is fiction or nonfiction.
> 4. **DECIDE** what type of literature it is.

DIRECTIONS:

Now, read the following selection and write on the lines whether it is *historical fiction*, *realistic fiction*, or *fantasy*. Underline the words that helped you decide. Explain why you made your choice.

It was very crowded on the *Mayflower*. Sarah knew that one person had died on the voyage already. She also knew that her mother had helped with the birth of a baby last night. It was almost as though one life had been taken and another given to make up for the loss.

_____

_____

_____

_____

Name _____ Date _____

POSSIBLE OR IMPOSSIBLE?

 **DIRECTIONS:**

Read the steps below.

> **Remember, To Respond to Forms of Literature:**
> 1. READ the selection carefully.
> 2. THINK about the people and places in the selection.
> 3. DECIDE if the selection is fiction or nonfiction.
> 4. DECIDE what type of literature it is.

Now, read each of these selections and fill in the answer circle in front of the choice that best identifies the literature.

1. Was it possible? Would Mr. Samuels let a girl ride for the Pony Express? I could feel the excitement rise in my stomach, but I was confident I could do the job.

This selection is _____.
Ⓐ historical fiction   Ⓑ realistic fiction   Ⓒ fantasy

2. It was Jim's first day in his new school. All summer he had been dreading this day. He wouldn't know anyone, and with his luck, not a person would speak to him all day. He knew he'd miss his teacher, too.

This selection is _____.
Ⓐ historical fiction   Ⓑ realistic fiction   Ⓒ fantasy

3. The prince and the princess each took a magic sword and fought the fearful dragon. They forced him back into his cave. As he disappeared into the dark depths, the townspeople crept out from the bushes where they had been hiding and thanked the prince and the princess for their bravery.

This selection is _____.
Ⓐ historical fiction   Ⓑ realistic fiction   Ⓒ fantasy

4. Daniel couldn't decide if the Indians were friendly or if they were from a hostile tribe. He decided to watch them from a distance for a little while longer. As he turned to tell his fellow travelers his decision, Jim, the youngest of the group, ran up to him and said, "Mr. Boone, I've brought a new friend to meet you." Beside Jim stood the Indian chief.

This selection is _____.
Ⓐ historical fiction   Ⓑ realistic fiction   Ⓒ fantasy

Forms of Literature

Name _____   Date _____

· ·

PERSONIFICATION

 **DIRECTIONS:**

Read this sentence and think about its meaning.

The clothes on the line danced in the wind.

What did you decide this sentence means? If you said that the wind is blowing the clothes around on the clothesline, then you understood the sentence.

Did you notice that the writer gave the clothes a human characteristic? The clothes are dancing. This makes the sentence more interesting, and the clothes seem real. When objects, ideas, places, and animals are given human characteristics, it is called *personification*. Personification is one kind of figurative language that helps the author create an exciting word picture in the reader's mind.

To Recognize Personification:
1. **READ the sentence carefully.**
2. **THINK about the meaning of the sentence.**
3. **NOTICE how personification creates a word picture and makes the sentence more interesting.**

Now, read each sentence below that uses personification and rewrite it without using personification.

1. The bushes hug the ground in our backyard.

_____

2. The sailboat danced gracefully past us.

_____

3. Winter delivered his cold, white present to the waiting ground.

_____

4. The tulip nodded her lovely head to the passing breeze.

_____

5. The broad, flat rock lay sunning itself by the stream.

_____

Name _____ Date _____

IT DID WHAT?

 **DIRECTIONS:**

Read the steps below.

> **Remember, To Recognize Personification:**
> 1. **READ the sentence carefully.**
> 2. **THINK about the meaning of the sentence.**
> 3. **NOTICE how personification creates a word picture and makes the sentence more interesting.**

Read each sentence and fill in the answer circle in front of the choice that has the same, or nearly the same, meaning as the sentence.

1. The tree fought the wind with its branches.
- Ⓐ A battle was being fought beneath the tree.
- Ⓑ The tree branches were moving in the wind.

2. The computer devoured information all day long.
- Ⓐ The computer was being given information all day.
- Ⓑ The computer ate the student's lunch.

3. The clock on the wall ordered the children on to their next class.
- Ⓐ It was time for the children to go to their next class.
- Ⓑ The principal had ordered the clock removed from the wall.

4. The sun peeked its head over the horizon and announced it was time to get up.
- Ⓐ Someone peeked around the door and said to get up.
- Ⓑ The sun came up, and the light awakened many people.

5. The fog crept silently into the valley.
- Ⓐ Animals were creeping into the valley.
- Ⓑ The fog came slowly into the valley.

6. The hikers left the meadow and were swallowed by the forest.
- Ⓐ The hikers disappeared among the forest trees.
- Ⓑ The forest ate the hikers.

7. The ruins refused to give up their secrets.
- Ⓐ People could not get the ruins to talk.
- Ⓑ People could not get enough clues from the ruins.

Name_____   Date_____

THAT'S WHAT YOU THINK!

 **DIRECTIONS:**

Read the steps below.

> **To Distinguish Between Fact and Opinion:**
> 1. **READ the statement carefully.**
> 2. **THINK about its meaning.**
> 3. **DECIDE whether it is a fact or an opinion.**

Now, read each story. Fill in the answer circle in front of the correct answer.

Poison ivy is a common, poisonous plant. It has three leaflets on each stem and white berries. Poison ivy can grow as a bush or as a vine. Its leaves are green and shiny in the summer. In the fall, they are a beautiful shade of red. Some people can have a severe reaction if they come into contact with any part of the plant. The poisonous juice is present in the leaves, stem, and flowers. Many people think that any plant with three leaves and white berries should be avoided to prevent possible poisoning.

1. Which one of the following is a statement of *opinion* supported by the story?
Ⓐ Poison ivy has three leaflets and white berries.
Ⓑ I think the poisonous juice causes swelling.
Ⓒ The leaves are a beautiful shade of red in the fall.
Ⓓ I believe that the berries are not poisonous.

The planet Venus was named for the goddess of beauty. It is a lovely name. Venus is the brightest object in the sky except for the sun and moon. It is the "morning star" or "evening star" that is often seen. Venus is never seen in the middle of the night. Some people think of it as a mysterious planet because its surface is always covered with clouds. Venus is about the size of Earth and is the closest of all the known planets to Earth.

2. Which one of the following is a statement of *fact* supported by the story?
Ⓐ Mars is brighter than Venus when viewed from Earth.
Ⓑ Venus is always covered with clouds, which hide the surface.
Ⓒ Some people think Venus is mysterious because of the cloud cover.
Ⓓ The temperature of Venus is much colder than Earth.

Go on to the next page.

THAT'S WHAT YOU THINK! (P. 2)

Read each story. Fill in the answer circle in front of the correct answer.

Captain Kidd was a horrible pirate who was eventually hanged for his crimes. He was once an ordinary seaman. The king of England sent him to capture pirates in the Red Sea and the Indian Ocean. No one heard from him for a while. Many people believed he was dead. Then, stories were heard that Captain Kidd had become a pirate himself. When he sailed into New York harbor, he was captured. He defended himself by saying the pirates made him become one of them.

3. Which one of the following is a statement of *opinion* supported by the story?
- Ⓐ The king of England sent Kidd to capture pirates.
- Ⓑ Many people thought he was unjustly hanged.
- Ⓒ I believe he was a soldier before becoming a pirate.
- Ⓓ When he didn't return, he was believed dead.

People learned to raise pigs long ago. Pigs are also called hogs, or swine. They are raised for their meat, fat, and skin. Many people think that pigs are very dirty, but they roll in the mud to cool their bodies and to avoid insects. Pigs are thought by many people to be very bright animals. They can be trained as pets, but it isn't done very often.

4. Which one of the following is a statement of *fact* supported by the story?
- Ⓐ Pigs are also called hogs, or swine.
- Ⓑ The meat of the pig is pork, ham, or lamb.
- Ⓒ The pig rolls in mud to soften its skin.
- Ⓓ Many people think that pigs are very clean.

Name_____ Date_____

IN MY OPINION...

 **DIRECTIONS:**

Read each story. Fill in the answer circle in front of the correct answer.

Crustaceans are animals with jointed legs and bodies and an outside covering that protects them. This covering does not grow with the animal, so it must occasionally be shed and a new one grown. Some crustaceans are the lobster, the crab, and the shrimp. Some people believe these are delicious foods. Other crustaceans, such as the tiny water flea, must be viewed through a microscope.

1. Which one of the following statements is an *opinion* supported by the story?
- Ⓐ Some people think that lobster is delicious.
- Ⓑ I don't think the shrimp is a crustacean.
- Ⓒ Crustaceans regularly shed their covering.
- Ⓓ The feelers on crustaceans are ugly.

Crater Lake is in the crater of a dead volcano. It is the most beautiful lake in the world. Its sides are covered with evergreens, and its water is a bright blue. The lake is about 2,000 feet deep. It is the deepest lake in the United States. The sides of the crater rise 2,000 feet above the lake's surface. It would be great if everyone could see Crater Lake.

2. Which one of the following statements is a *fact* supported by the story?
- Ⓐ The sides of the crater are treeless.
- Ⓑ The lava sides of the crater are twisted.
- Ⓒ The bright blue water makes the lake beautiful.
- Ⓓ Crater Lake is the deepest lake in the United States.

Mr. and Mrs. Phillips have two children. Everyone thinks that the boys look like their dad. They have dark hair and eyes and are tall for their ages. Sometimes, the Phillips vacation on Padre Island. They think it is beautiful there. They believe that it is easier to survive the long Minnesota winters if they get away to a warm place in December. Grandma and Grandpa feel their grandchildren should stay in Minnesota for the holidays with them. Instead of canceling their next vacation, the Phillips are taking the grandparents along, too.

3. Which one of the following is a statement of *opinion* supported by the story?
- Ⓐ People think that the boys look like their dad.
- Ⓑ Next year, the grandparents are going to Padre Island.
- Ⓒ The Phillips boys have beautiful blond hair.
- Ⓓ The grandparents think they should fly when they go.

Go on to the next page.

Fact and Opinion
Study Skills 6, SV 8054-5

IN MY OPINION... (P. 2)

DIRECTIONS:

Read each story. Fill in the answer circle in front of the correct answer.

Many geologists, or earth scientists, believe the seven continents were once one large continent. This idea is not a new one. A German scientist suggested this idea about sixty years ago, but the idea was laughed at by other scientists. When people look at the shape of the continents, they often think they might fit together. This is one part of the argument for a supercontinent. Another piece of evidence is matching fossils that have been found in Africa and South America. Also, tropical plant fossils have been found in Antarctica. The idea of floating continents is a very interesting one.

4. Which of the following is a statement of *fact* supported by the story?
  Ⓐ The continents are moving on plates.
  Ⓑ This idea is very interesting.
  Ⓒ The idea of a supercontinent is a new one.
  Ⓓ Matching fossils have provided evidence.

Moose are the largest of all antlered animals. The Alaskan moose is the largest moose of all, some weighing as much as 1,800 pounds. Some Alaskan bull moose have been measured at 7 1/2 feet at the shoulder. Their antlers reach to 10 feet above the ground. These antlers can weigh 95 pounds and reach widths of 6 feet and more. The size of these animals is amazing.

5. Which of the following is a statement of *opinion* supported by the story?
  Ⓐ Moose are the largest of all antlered animals.
  Ⓑ The size of these animals is amazing.
  Ⓒ Their antlers reach to 10 feet above the ground.
  Ⓓ The Alaskan moose is the largest moose of all.

Fact and Opinion

Name_____ Date_____

· ·

CAUSE AND EFFECT

 **DIRECTIONS:**

Read this sentence and think about what happened.

The child had a fever because she had the flu.

What part of this sentence tells what happened? Yes, *the child had a fever* is what happened. Why did it happen? It happened *because she had the flu.*

Sentences like the one above are important to understand because they often answer the question "WHY?" in a story. The part of the sentence that tells "WHY" is the *cause.* It is what makes something else happen. The part of the sentence that tells "WHAT HAPPENED" is the *effect.* It is what results or happens.

Let's look at the sentence again.

The child had a fever because she had the flu.
     effect   cause

Do you notice a word that gives us a clue as to which part of the sentence is the cause? Yes, the word *because* is a clue word. Here are some clue words that will help you find the cause and effect.

CLUE WORDS

cause	effect
1. because	1. therefore
2. since	2. thus
	3. so
	4. as a result

Look for these words to help you decide which part of the sentence is the cause and which is the effect.

> **To Understand Cause and Effect:**
> **1. READ the sentence carefully.**
> **2. LOOK for clue words.**
> **3. DECIDE which part of the sentence is the cause and which part is the effect.**
> **4. USE that information to help answer "WHY?"**

In this sentence, draw a circle around the cause and underline the effect.

Because her shoes were too tight, her feet hurt.

Go on to the next page.

CAUSE AND EFFECT (P. 2)

DIRECTIONS:

In these sentences, draw a circle around the cause and underline the effect.

1. I like to go to the circus because of the clowns.

2. Since you gave me a dollar, I can buy the candy.

3. It was hot outside; therefore, Joe wore his shorts.

4. Jill forgot to shut the door, so the dog got out.

5. Since Sarah has a computer, we worked at her house.

6. Ronnie liked the cupcakes because they were chocolate.

7. Kay didn't have a pencil since she loaned hers to me.

8. Because Mom called us for supper, we couldn't play anymore.

9. Mom lit the candles because the electricity was out.

10. The invention is mine; therefore, he can't take the credit.

Follow the directions as you write your own sentences. Remember to start each sentence with a capital letter and end it with the correct punctuation.

11. Write a sentence telling why you didn't remember my birthday last week. Use the word *because*.

_____

_____

12. Write a sentence telling why you missed the school bus.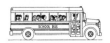

_____

_____

Name_____ Date_____

••

WHAT MADE IT HAPPEN?

 **DIRECTIONS:**

Read the steps below.

> **To Understand Cause and Effect:**
> 1. **READ the sentence carefully.**
> 2. **LOOK for clue words.**
> 3. **DECIDE which part of the sentence is the cause and which part is the effect.**

Read these selections. Fill in the answer circle in front of the choice that best completes each sentence.

Dad decided to have a garden this year because vegetables are so expensive at the grocery store. He thought it would save us a lot of money and time. Boy! Was he wrong! Since he bought so many strange and exotic kinds of seeds, our bill was enormous. You wouldn't believe the time we spent on that garden. We weeded, watered, and sprayed for several hours every day. Was it worth it? My dad says it was a learning experience; and because the yard was already torn up for the garden, Dad put in a basketball court for me. I think it was worth it!

1. Because vegetables were so expensive, Dad _____.
   Ⓐ decided to have a garden this year
   Ⓑ took out a loan at the bank
   Ⓒ sold strange and exotic kinds of seeds
   Ⓓ hired a gardener to raise vegetables

2. Dad put in a basketball court for me because _____.
   Ⓐ he wanted me to get a scholarship
   Ⓑ the yard was already torn up
   Ⓒ it was my birthday
   Ⓓ I needed a learning experience

Noise is around us all of the time. Many people think that noise pollution is becoming a problem because there are so many things in our environment that make noise. Too much noise can cause deafness, sleeplessness, irritability, and even pain.

3. People think noise pollution is becoming a problem because _____.
   Ⓐ there are many noisy things in our environment
   Ⓑ people are becoming more irritable every day
   Ⓒ deafness has developed in many city dwellers
   Ⓓ doctors are seeing an increase in headaches

Go on to the next page.

Cause and Effect
Study Skills 6, SV 8054-5

WHAT MADE IT HAPPEN? (P. 2)

DIRECTIONS:

Read each story. Fill in the answer circle in front of the choice that best completes each sentence.

Our solar system has one sun. We call it a solar system because the word *sol* means sun in Latin. There are at least eight other planets besides Earth that travel in orbits around the sun. We say at least eight because that is how many we know of at this time. There might, in fact, be more beyond Pluto that we cannot see.

4. Because the word *sol* means sun in Latin, _____.
- Ⓐ we call our sun and its planets the solar system
- Ⓑ there are at least eight other planets besides Earth
- Ⓒ there might be other planets beyond Pluto
- Ⓓ our solar system has one sun

Robert Louis Stevenson was a famous author who was born in Scotland. He had studied to be an engineer and a lawyer. He wasn't able to do these things because of poor health. He began to write for magazines instead. He wrote *Treasure Island* because he wanted to entertain his young stepson. He also wrote *Kidnapped* and *The Strange Case of Dr. Jekyll and Mr. Hyde*. He died in the Samoan Islands. The natives honored him; and, as a result, they buried him as they would a chief. They called him "teller of tales."

5. Because of poor health, Robert Louis Stevenson _____.
- Ⓐ wanted to entertain his stepson
- Ⓑ couldn't be an engineer or lawyer
- Ⓒ was called "teller of tales"
- Ⓓ wrote *Treasure Island*

6. The natives buried Robert Louis Stevenson as a chief because he _____.
- Ⓐ wrote *Kidnapped*
- Ⓑ was a lawyer
- Ⓒ was born in Samoa
- Ⓓ was honored by them

Cause and Effect

Name_____   Date_____

THE WHAT AND THE WHY

DIRECTIONS:

Read the steps below.

> **To Understand Cause and Effect:**
> 1. READ the sentence carefully.
> 2. LOOK for the clue words.
> 3. DECIDE which part of the sentence is the cause and which part is the effect.

Now, read each story. Fill in the answer circle in front of the choice that best completes each sentence.

Over 2,000 years ago, Plato said there had been another continent called Atlantis. He said it had sunk because of an earthquake. Scientists haven't found any evidence that Plato's idea is true, so it is considered by most people to be untrue. Some people, however, continue to believe in Atlantis.

1. Plato said that Atlantis sank because of _____.
Ⓐ volcanic eruptions
Ⓑ too little evidence
Ⓒ an earthquake
Ⓓ a solar eclipse

2. Because scientists haven't found any evidence, they _____.
Ⓐ continue looking for proof
Ⓑ call Plato a liar
Ⓒ study earthquakes
Ⓓ believe the idea is untrue

Ms. Rogers built a fence around her backyard so her dog could exercise safely. Because the fencing would be very expensive, she thought carefully before spending her money. After the five-foot fence was completed, the dog was allowed to run freely in the yard. Unfortunately, the fence is now useless because the dog has learned to jump over it.

3. Ms. Rogers thought carefully about building the fence because _____.
Ⓐ she knew the dog would jump over
Ⓑ her yard wouldn't be easy to mow
Ⓒ her dog could exercise safely
Ⓓ the fence would be expensive

Go on to the next page.

THE WHAT AND THE WHY (P. 2)

DIRECTIONS:

Read each story. Fill in the answer circle in front of the choice that best completes each sentence.

Coffee is a popular drink in the United States. It is made from the seeds of the coffee plant. These seeds are called coffee "beans" because they look like beans to us. Coffee is grown in a warm climate because it cannot stand any frost at all. Most coffee plantations are in South or Central America. Coffee contains the drug caffeine, which is a stimulant. It is called a stimulant because it increases body activity. Many people drink coffee to wake themselves up in the morning.

4. Because coffee cannot stand any frost, it is _____.
- Ⓐ kept in heated buildings
- Ⓑ called a stimulant
- Ⓒ grown in a warm climate
- Ⓓ used as a morning drink

5. The seeds of the coffee plant are called coffee "beans" because _____.
- Ⓐ bean is the Spanish word for seed
- Ⓑ coffee contains the drug caffeine
- Ⓒ the seeds look like beans to us
- Ⓓ coffee is grown in South America

Bonita's mother was worried about her because her school work was not as good as it had been. Bonita seemed to try hard, but she was making mistakes in work done at school. Her teacher suggested that Bonita have her eyes examined because sometimes poor eyesight can cause this kind of problem. Bonita was nervous because she had never been to an eye doctor. After the tests, the doctor told Bonita that she needed glasses. Bonita is now amazed at the things she can see because of the glasses.

6. Because she had never been to an eye doctor, Bonita _____.
- Ⓐ was nervous
- Ⓑ ran away
- Ⓒ needed glasses
- Ⓓ was amazed

Cause and Effect

Name _____   Date _____

THE REASON WHY

 **DIRECTIONS:**

Read each story. Fill in the answer circle in front of the choice that best completes each sentence.

The Pueblo Indians of today have as their ancestors the cliff dwellers. They were called cliff dwellers because their homes were built on the side of cliffs. These homes were built over 200 years before Christopher Columbus landed in America. The cliff dwellers were farmers who raised corn and beans. The cliff dwellings were easy to defend against enemies because they were so hard to reach. About 700 years ago, the cliff dwellers left their homes. Some historians believe they left because of a drought, a long period with no rain. No one really knows why these remarkable homes were abandoned.

1. Because the cliff dwellings were so hard to reach, they were _____.
- Ⓐ abandoned
- Ⓑ easy to defend
- Ⓒ without rain
- Ⓓ Pueblo Indians

2. Some historians believe the cliff dwellers left because _____.
- Ⓐ the Pueblo Indians attacked
- Ⓑ the homes were hard to reach
- Ⓒ Columbus landed in America
- Ⓓ there was a period of drought

Blanca had practiced all spring because she wanted to do a good job on the softball team this summer. Her brother had pitched to her so she could practice batting. She had played catch to improve the way she handled the ball. Her coach, Mrs. Wilson, noticed the big improvement. Because Blanca played so well, she was selected as the Most Valuable Player at the end of the season.

3. Because she wanted to improve her batting, Blanca _____.
- Ⓐ played catch all spring
- Ⓑ bought a new, expensive bat
- Ⓒ had her brother pitch to her
- Ⓓ asked Mrs. Wilson for help

Go on to the next page.

Cause and Effect

THE REASON WHY (P. 2)

DIRECTIONS:

Read each story. Fill in the answer circle in front of the choice that best completes each sentence.

Oranges are the most popular citrus fruits. They get the name *citrus* from the fruit citron found near the Mediterranean Sea. The orange, like other citrus fruits, is covered with a leathery peel and is divided into sections inside. Some oranges are for eating; others are raised for their juice. Juice oranges are an important crop because so many of them are used to produce frozen orange juice. The orange tree is beautiful because of its shiny leaves, white blossoms, and golden fruit.

4. Because juice oranges are used in producing frozen orange juice, they are _____.
- Ⓐ an important crop
- Ⓑ called citrus fruits
- Ⓒ divided into sections
- Ⓓ frozen immediately

5. The orange tree is beautiful because it _____.
- Ⓐ comes from the Mediterranean Sea
- Ⓑ has lovely leaves, blossoms, and fruit
- Ⓒ is divided into sections
- Ⓓ never loses its shiny leaves

Amanda had to move into an upstairs bedroom because her mother was having a baby. The baby needed Amanda's old room because it was closer to Mom and Dad's bedroom, and the baby could be taken care of more easily. The new room was to be special and more grown-up than her old room. Amanda's parents wanted Amanda to feel important because sometimes older brothers and sisters feel jealous when a new baby arrives. They loved Amanda and didn't want her to feel bad about giving up her room near theirs.

6. Because her mother was having a baby, Amanda _____.
- Ⓐ was already jealous
- Ⓑ learned to change diapers
- Ⓒ cleaned the house
- Ⓓ had to move to an upstairs bedroom

Cause and Effect
Study Skills 6, SV 8054-5

Name_____ Date_____

PREDICTING OUTCOMES

 DIRECTIONS:

Read the following story and decide what happens next.

Janet had been working all day. She was not finished, but it was time for her friend's party.

Did you decide that Janet would get ready for the party? If you did, then you were right! Using the information in the story, it would make sense to predict that Janet would do exactly that. To *predict* means to tell what will happen next.

What if we added this to the story? Would it change your prediction?

Janet had to have the work done by tomorrow, or she would lose her job.

Now you would probably predict that Janet would not go to the party. Your prediction changed when you got new information.

> **To Predict Future Outcomes or Actions:**
> 1. **READ** the story carefully.
> 2. **THINK** about the information in the story.
> 3. **DECIDE** what will happen next.
> 4. **CHANGE** your prediction, if necessary, when you get new information.

Read the following story and predict what will happen next.

Patricia's mother could not get the car started, and Patricia would soon be late for school. Her friend, Tara, lived around the corner, and her dad took her to school every day.

1. What will happen next?

_____

Now, read this information and change your prediction, if necessary.

When Patricia called Tara, she had already left for school. School was less than a mile away, and it was a pretty day.

2. What will Patricia do next?

_____

Go on to the next page.

PREDICTING OUTCOMES (P. 2)

DIRECTIONS:

Read each story and answer the questions.

Jake was walking home from ball practice. He was hot, and his clothes were wet with sweat. As he neared Bryan Park, he remembered there was a water fountain by the swings.

3. What will Jake do next?

_____

As Jake walked toward the fountain, he heard his little brother yell to him from the car. Mom had come to pick him up, and his brother was holding up a frosty can of juice.

4. Now, what will Jake do?

_____

On the first day of school, Tina walked into the classroom a little late. All of the seats had been taken except the one up front by the teacher's desk.

5. What will Tina do next?

_____

The Davis family was having a picnic down by the lakeshore. It was their last night in the cottage before returning home. Dark, threatening clouds were gathering in the west, and the wind was becoming gusty.

6. What will the Davis family do next?

_____

There was a fireplace in the cottage, and the family had planned on roasting hot dogs and marshmallows, anyway.

7. Now, what will the Davis family do?

_____

50

Name _____   Date _____

WHAT WILL HAPPEN NEXT?

DIRECTIONS:

Read the steps below.

> **Remember, To Predict Future Outcomes or Actions:**
> 1. **READ** the story carefully.
> 2. **THINK** about the information in the story.
> 3. **DECIDE** what will happen next.
> 4. **CHANGE** your prediction, if necessary, when you get new information.

Read these stories. Fill in the answer circle in front of the choice that best completes each sentence.

Ralph wants to visit the southern part of the United States. He has no money for an expensive vacation. Ralph's Uncle John lives in Dallas and has a large house.

1. Ralph will probably _____.
- Ⓐ ask Uncle John if he can stay with him in Dallas
- Ⓑ get a loan from the bank for his vacation
- Ⓒ take a vacation nearer to home instead of Texas
- Ⓓ stay home and read books about Texas

Joan has been having problems getting her dog to obey. He is hard to control when she walks him around the neighborhood. While reading the paper, Joan sees an advertisement for a dog obedience school.

2. Joan will probably _____.
- Ⓐ sell her dog
- Ⓑ call the school
- Ⓒ stop taking walks
- Ⓓ buy another dog

It is a beautiful spring day. Mr. Ellis has a new car with a sunroof, and it is his day off.

3. Mr. Ellis will probably _____.
- Ⓐ stay inside and do housework
- Ⓑ watch baseball on television
- Ⓒ take a ride in his new car
- Ⓓ go to a movie and then shop

Go on to the next page.

WHAT WILL HAPPEN NEXT? (P. 2)

DIRECTIONS:

Read these stories. Fill in the answer circle in front of the choice that best completes each sentence.

The Johnsons have two children, Jessica and Justin. Susan Craig has been their baby-sitter for the past two years. They like her and so do the children. The past few times the Johnsons have called Susan to baby-sit, she has been too busy. Their anniversary is this Saturday, and, once again, Susan can't come. They know about a boy who baby-sits and has been recommended by friends.

4. The Johnsons will probably _____.
- Ⓐ stay home and forget about celebrating
- Ⓑ call the boy and ask him to baby-sit
- Ⓒ take the children to a neighbor for the night
- Ⓓ let the children stay by themselves

Pete has been thinking about buying a cassette by his favorite singer, but he's not sure that it's worth the money His friend, Steve, has the cassette.

5. Pete will probably _____.
- Ⓐ buy the cassette and take a chance that it is good
- Ⓑ sell his stereo and forget about buying cassettes
- Ⓒ ask Steve to give him his cassette
- Ⓓ listen to Steve's cassette and decide about buying

The wagon train had been crossing the prairie for a month. Now a decision had to be made whether to take the northern or southern route across the mountains. This time of year, snow in the northern pass would probably make travel difficult, if not impossible.

6. The wagon train will probably _____.
- Ⓐ wait until later in the year to cross the mountains
- Ⓑ take the northern pass and be prepared for trouble
- Ⓒ take the southern pass to avoid the snow in the north
- Ⓓ go back to St. Louis and forget about going west

Name _____ Date _____

GENERALIZATIONS

 **DIRECTIONS:**

Read the following story and think about its meaning.

There are four people in my family. Three of us have names that start with "J." Most of our names start with "J."

If you look carefully at the first two sentences, you will notice that both of them state facts about the family. The third sentence makes a statement that ties together the facts already stated. That last sentence is called a *generalization.* To make a generalization, you need more than one fact.

Certain words are clues to finding generalizations. Here are some of them:

some	all
most	none
many	always
several	every
a few	
often	

The clue words in the second column must be used carefully. They can only be used when the generalization is true in **all** cases.

> **To Make a Generalization:**
> 1. **READ the facts carefully.**
> 2. **THINK about how they are related.**
> 3. **MAKE a statement that ties them together. Use one of the clue words.**

Now, read the facts and make generalizations.

The cardinal is brightly colored; so is the blue jay.

1. _____

My father is a kindergarten teacher. My mother teaches chemistry.

2. _____

In our class at school, we have 26 students. Twenty of us do not wear glasses.

3. _____

Generalizations

Study Skills 6, SV 8054-5

• •

GENERALLY SPEAKING

 **DIRECTIONS:**

Read the steps below.

Remember, To Make a Generalization:
1. **READ the facts carefully.**
2. **THINK about how they are related.**
3. **MAKE a statement that ties them together. Use one of the clue words.**

Read the facts. Fill in the answer circle in front of the statement that is the best generalization.

Insects have six legs. The ladybug is an insect.

1. Which statement is a valid or true generalization?
   Ⓐ Some ladybugs are insects.
   Ⓑ All ladybugs have six legs.
   Ⓒ Many ladybugs are not insects.

Ryan loves pizza. Sheila loves it, too. Cindy hates pizza.

2. Which statement is a valid or true generalization?
   Ⓐ Everyone likes pizza.
   Ⓑ No one likes pizza.
   Ⓒ Some people like pizza.

There are three girls in my family: Nancy, Judy, and Sally. I play the piano, Nancy plays the violin, and Sally plays the flute.

3. Which statement is a valid or true generalization?
   Ⓐ Some of the girls in my family play an instrument.
   Ⓑ Most of the girls in my family play an instrument.
   Ⓒ All of the girls in my family play an instrument.

Go on to the next page.

GENERALLY SPEAKING (P. 2)

DIRECTIONS:

Read the facts. Fill in the answer circle in front of the statement that is the best generalization.

Vertebrates are animals with backbones. Invertebrates are animals without backbones. Out of about 1,000,000 kinds of animals, only about 50,000 have backbones.

4. Which statement is a valid or true generalization?
- Ⓐ Most animals are invertebrates.
- Ⓑ Most animals are vertebrates.
- Ⓒ All animals have backbones.

Jeff has his own computer. Rebecca does, too. They are the only people in our class who have one at home.

5. Which statement is a valid or true generalization?
- Ⓐ A few children have a computer.
- Ⓑ No one has a computer.
- Ⓒ Most children have a computer.

The Venus flytrap is a plant that eats insects. Pitcher plants also trap insects.

6. Which statement is a valid or true generalization?
- Ⓐ All plants eat insects.
- Ⓑ Some plants eat insects.
- Ⓒ No plant eats insects.

Juanita has 100 books in her own personal library at home. Twenty-five of them are books of poetry, ten are adventure stories, and the rest are fiction and nonfiction about horses.

7. Which statement is a valid or true generalization?
- Ⓐ All of Juanita's books are about horses.
- Ⓑ A few of Juanita's books are about horses.
- Ⓒ Most of Juanita's books are about horses.

Name_____   Date_____

• •

JUDGMENTS

Every day you are given a lot of information from radio, television, magazines, and people. It is important to be able to decide what is true and important to you. This is called making a judgment.

 **DIRECTIONS:**

Read these statements and think about the meaning of each.

Reading books can increase your knowledge.

Reading can cause warts.

I think reading is fun; at least it is for me.

In the sentences above, three statements are made about reading. What do you think about each one? The first statement is true. It can be proved to be a fact. The second statement is false. It doesn't seem possible from what we know about reading. The third statement is a valid opinion. This means that even though it is an opinion, it is backed up with facts. It is true for that person.

Reading books can increase your knowledge. (true)

Reading can cause warts. (false)

I think reading is fun; at least it is for me. (valid opinion)

> **To Make a Judgment:**
> **1. READ or LISTEN to the statement carefully.**
> **2. THINK about the meaning of the statement.**
> **3. DECIDE whether it is true, false, or a valid opinion.**

Read each of these statements and fill in the answer circle in front of the correct answer.

1. Encyclopedias contain fiction stories by famous authors.
Ⓐ true
Ⓑ false
Ⓒ valid opinion

2. Oranges contain vitamin C.
Ⓐ true
Ⓑ false
Ⓒ valid opinion

Judgments

Name_____ Date_____

HOW'S YOUR JUDGMENT?

DIRECTIONS:

Read the steps below.

> **Remember, To Make a Judgment:**
> 1. **READ or LISTEN to the statement carefully.**
> 2. **THINK about the meaning of the statement.**
> 3. **DECIDE whether it is true, false, or a valid opinion.**

Read each of these statements and fill in the answer circle in front of the correct answer.

1. The most popular hobby in the United States is raising cucumbers.
- Ⓐ true
- Ⓑ false
- Ⓒ valid opinion

2. Rain has been known to shrink people.
- Ⓐ true
- Ⓑ false
- Ⓒ valid opinion

3. Smoking is bad for your health.
- Ⓐ true
- Ⓑ false
- Ⓒ valid opinion

4. I think that dogs are the best pets.
- Ⓐ true
- Ⓑ false
- Ⓒ valid opinion

5. In 1959, Hawaii became the fiftieth state.
- Ⓐ true
- Ⓑ false
- Ⓒ valid opinion

Go on to the next page.

Study Skills 6, SV 8054-5

• •

HOW'S YOUR JUDGMENT? (P. 2)

DIRECTIONS:

Read each of these statements and fill in the answer circle in front of the correct answer.

6. The Mississippi River flows by Mississippi.
- Ⓐ true
- Ⓑ false
- Ⓒ valid opinion

7. In my opinion, watching television is a waste of time.
- Ⓐ true
- Ⓑ false
- Ⓒ valid opinion

8. People will get the measles if they eat strawberries.
- Ⓐ true
- Ⓑ false
- Ⓒ valid opinion

9. Green plants can use the sun's energy to make food.
- Ⓐ true
- Ⓑ false
- Ⓒ valid opinion

10. The Grand Canyon is the most beautiful place I've ever seen.
- Ⓐ true
- Ⓑ false
- Ⓒ valid opinion

11. Listening to rock music makes your hair grow faster.
- Ⓐ true
- Ⓑ false
- Ⓒ valid opinion

• •

GETTING THE MAIN IDEA

 **DIRECTIONS:**

Read this selection and think about its main idea.

The great Mississippi River divides the 48-state part of the United States into two parts. It runs from near Canada to the Gulf of Mexico. It is more than a mile wide in some places. Many large and important rivers flow into it. A huge amount of water flows down the Mississippi.

What is its main idea? If you decided that the main idea was how large the Mississippi River is, then you were right. Finding the main idea is finding the most important idea.

The main idea cannot be a statement that is not true. We could not say the main idea was that the Mississippi is the largest river in the United States. Even if that is true, the selection doesn't say that. We also couldn't say that the main idea was that the Mississippi divides the 48-state part of the United States into four parts. The selection says two parts.

The main idea cannot be a statement that is only a detail. We could not say that the main idea was that the Mississippi River runs from near Canada to the Gulf of Mexico. Even though that is true, it does not tell us the overall idea of the selection.

> **To Find the Main Idea:**
> 1. **READ** the passage carefully.
> 2. **THINK** about the passage and its meaning.
> 3. **DECIDE** on the main idea.

Now, read the passage. Then fill in the answer circle in front of the choice that best completes the sentence and answer the question.

The mongoose is a small meat-eating mammal. It eats snakes and is quick enough to avoid the snake if it strikes. Its speed enables it to kill the king cobra, one of the most poisonous snakes. The mongoose is one of the world's most active animals. With its quickness, it is also a successful hunter of rats, mice, and wild birds.

1. The story is mainly about the _____.
   Ⓐ world's most poisonous snake
   Ⓑ slow and lazy mongoose
   Ⓒ hunting skills of the mongoose
   Ⓓ story "Rikki-tikki-tavi"

2. How do you know?

_____

Go on to the next page.

Main Idea

GETTING THE MAIN IDEA (P. 2)

DIRECTIONS:

Read each passage. Then fill in the answer circle in front of the choice that best completes the sentence, and answer the question.

Peter had worked with his dad fixing things around the house even before he had started school. He knew how to take almost anything apart and put it back together correctly. He had fixed his Aunt Jennifer's car when it was making a horrible grinding sound. When his sister's stereo speaker wasn't making any sound, Peter tinkered with it for an hour and soon had it working better than ever. Everyone in the family and in his neighborhood knew whom to come to when anything needed fixing.

3. The story is mainly about _____.
Ⓐ fixing the lawn mower
Ⓑ a car fixed for an aunt
Ⓒ breaking a speaker
Ⓓ a talented young man

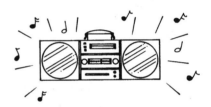

4. How did you know?

_____

Stephen Foster composed songs, such as "My Old Kentucky Home," that we still sing today. Even though he was a talented writer of songs, he had a very unhappy life. He died at the age of 38, homeless, without friends, and almost penniless. In fact, he made very little money from any of the 200 songs he wrote.

5. The story is mainly about the _____.
Ⓐ unhappy life of Stephen Foster
Ⓑ 100 songs by Stephen Foster
Ⓒ way a composer gets ideas
Ⓓ death of Stephen Foster at 38

6. How did you know?

_____

Name _____ Date _____

WHAT'S THE BIG IDEA?

Read these steps.

> **Remember, To Find the Main Idea:**
> 1. READ the passage carefully.
> 2. THINK about the passage and its meaning.
> 3. DECIDE on the main idea.

Read each passage. Fill in the answer circle in front of the choice that best completes the sentence.

Manuel knew exactly what he had to do Saturday. He got up early and fixed his mom a breakfast fit for a queen. He waxed her car and cleaned his room without being told. When she left to go to the store, he hurried to the kitchen and baked her birthday cake. He carefully counted out the candles and stuck them into the icing. He knew she thought no one would remember her birthday. Had he done enough to make her day special?

1. The story is mainly about _____.
- Ⓐ fixing a birthday cake
- Ⓑ celebrating a fortieth birthday
- Ⓒ counting birthday candles
- Ⓓ remembering a special day

The whale is often mistaken for a fish instead of a mammal. The whale breathes air, has hair on parts of its body, and is warm-blooded. Baby whales, called calves, get milk from their mother's body. These are all characteristics of mammals.

2. The story is mainly about _____.
- Ⓐ baby whales called calves
- Ⓑ whales being mammals
- Ⓒ habits of the blue whale
- Ⓓ the whale's blood

Go on to the next page.

WHAT'S THE BIG IDEA? (P. 2)

DIRECTIONS:

Read each passage. Fill in the answer circle in front of the choice that best completes the sentence.

The paper wasp and the white-faced hornet build their nests out of paper. The yellow jacket, another kind of wasp, builds big nests in the ground. The potter wasp builds little jug-like nests on twigs, and the mud dauber builds a mud nest with many rooms. The cuckoo wasp doesn't build a nest. It lays eggs in the mud dauber's nest when the mud dauber is away.

3. The story is mainly about the _____.
- Ⓐ lazy, tricky cuckoo wasp
- Ⓑ many kinds of wasp nests
- Ⓒ asps living in colonies
- Ⓓ white-faced hornet

Maria had 27 ceramic horses on her blue painted shelves. She had horse pictures on all four walls of her room. When Maria had to write a story for school, she always wrote about how she wanted a horse, about a magic horse, or about the many kinds of horses. She had four shirts with horses on them, and she named her dog Trigger.

4. The story is mainly about a _____.

- Ⓐ magic horse called Trigger
- Ⓑ room decorated with horses
- Ⓒ girl who really loves horses
- Ⓓ blue painted shelf

Some artists draw pictures that look like real people and things. Others paint designs full of color and shape, but without anything that can be recognized. Many artists work with yarns, grasses, or clay. Some work with metal, stone, or even trash. What other materials have you seen artists use?

5. The story is mainly about the _____.

- Ⓐ different ways artists express themselves
- Ⓑ kinds of pictures that cannot be recognized
- Ⓒ use of colored glass in making designs
- Ⓓ artist needing to know how to draw people

Main Idea

GET TO THE POINT

 **DIRECTIONS:**

Read the steps below.

> **To Find the Main Idea:**
> 1. READ the passage carefully.
> 2. THINK about the passage and its meaning.
> 3. DECIDE on the main idea.

Now, read each story. Fill in the answer circle in front of the correct answer.

In the early days of the United States, a letter was often delivered by a traveler who happened to be going in the right direction. It might have changed hands many times. American Indians were sometimes good letter carriers, as were captains of ships. Many letters were left at a tavern near the desired destination, and they stayed there until someone picked them up.

1. This story is mainly about _____.
   Ⓐ captains of ships delivering mail   Ⓑ the first postmaster general
   Ⓒ mail delivery in early England   Ⓓ early mail delivery in the United States

It was Saturday and that meant Mom was sleeping late, so Maria crept into the kitchen. She got out the peanut butter, bread, and jelly. She made herself two thick sandwiches and settled down happily in front of the television.

2. This story is mainly about _____.
   Ⓐ asking Mom to make breakfast   Ⓑ watching television on Friday
   Ⓒ making a mess in the kitchen   Ⓓ making Saturday breakfast for one

Many people collect seashells. Shells have been used for money by people of the world. Some shells are used for decoration. Some animals are fed ground-up shells, and sometimes ground shells are added to soil to improve its quality.

3. This story is mainly about _____.
   Ⓐ using shells for game markers   Ⓑ the many uses of seashells
   Ⓒ feeding animals ground shells   Ⓓ how shells can ruin soil quality

Go on to the next page.

Main Idea

GET TO THE POINT (P. 2)

DIRECTIONS:

Read each story. Fill in the answer circle in front of the correct answer.

Roger had a collection of leaves that he had made in fourth grade. He also had a stamp collection and a terrific baseball card collection. Now, he was looking for coins minted the year he was born. The only collection that his parents had interfered with was when he was five and had started an ant collection. The ants had escaped and headed for the kitchen.

4. This story is mainly about _____.
  Ⓐ collecting things for school
  Ⓑ a football card collection
  Ⓒ Roger's many collections
  Ⓓ parents' interference in hobbies

Marcia pulled her scarf tighter around her face. Her toes felt numb inside her boots, and her fingers, curled inside their mittens, were losing all feeling, too. The wind pushed at her back, helping her on her way. Unfortunately, on the walk back home, she'd have to face that biting wind.

5. This story is mainly about _____.
  Ⓐ staying warm and cozy in the winter cold
  Ⓑ a biting wind making the walk difficult
  Ⓒ feeling cold on a walk in the winter wind
  Ⓓ walking to Grandma's house in the winter

Some breeds of sheep raised in the United States are the Merino, Hampshire, and Cheviot. The Karakul, also called a fat-tail sheep, is found in Asia. Wild sheep are found in Asia, northern Africa, and southern Europe. The bighorn, found in the Rocky Mountains, is another wild breed.

6. This story is mainly about _____.
  Ⓐ various breeds of sheep
  Ⓑ raising sheep for wool
  Ⓒ sheep in the United States
  Ⓓ having no more wild sheep

Main Idea

CONTEXT CLUES

**DIRECTIONS:**

Read the following sentence and think about the meaning of the underlined word.

In my <u>judgment,</u> or opinion, the picture doesn't look good hanging there.

How can you decide on the meaning of a word that is not known to you? In the sentence above, there was a clue to the meaning of the word *judgment.* That clue, called a context clue, was in the sentence itself. The sentence said, "... *judgment,* or opinion ...." If you read sentences carefully, you will often find context clues to help you understand the meaning of new words.

It is important not to let an unknown word stop you when reading. Do some detective work and look for those context clues.

> **To Use Context Clues:**
> 1. **READ** the sentence or sentences carefully.
> 2. **THINK** about the meaning of what you have read.
> 3. **LOOK** for context clues that can help you.
> 4. **DECIDE** on a possible meaning for the new word.

Now, read these sentences, decide on a meaning for the underlined word, and write it on the line. Remember to use context clues.

1. Food is a <u>necessity</u> for life.

_____

2. Jim's leg <u>fracture</u> caused him to be in a cast for six weeks.

_____

3. My sister looks like Mom, but I don't <u>resemble</u> her at all.

_____

4. The heat and humidity made the day too <u>sultry</u> to work in the garden.

_____

Go on to the next page.

Name _____   Date _____

• •

CONTEXT CLUES (P. 2)

 **DIRECTIONS:**

Read the steps below.

> **To Use Context Clues:**
> 1. **READ** the sentence or sentences carefully.
> 2. **THINK** about the meaning of what you have read.
> 3. **LOOK** for context clues that can help you.
> 4. **DECIDE** on a possible meaning for the new word.

Read each sentence. Choose the best meaning for the underlined word. Fill in the answer circle in front of the correct answer.

5. His father felt he made a major <u>concession</u> when he allowed Josh to use the car.
Ⓐ privilege to sell
Ⓑ acknowledged a point
Ⓒ oil painting on cloth
Ⓓ traveling in a train

6. The workers presented their employer with a <u>grievance</u> about the unfair practices in hiring.
Ⓐ award or trophy for excellence
Ⓑ large piece of furniture
Ⓒ complaint against a wrong
Ⓓ imaginary small creature

7. The wine steward sniffed the wine to check the <u>bouquet</u> and stated it was excellent.
Ⓐ a label of ingredients
Ⓑ the aroma or odor
Ⓒ a bunch of flowers
Ⓓ a colorful picture

Name_____ Date_____

IT'S IN THE CONTEXT

DIRECTIONS:

Read each sentence. Choose the best meaning for the underlined word. Fill in the answer circle in front of the correct answer.

1. The baseball flew like a <u>missile</u>, or rocket, toward the waiting batter.

   Ⓐ softly floating object
   Ⓑ an object launched at a target
   Ⓒ awkward animal with horns
   Ⓓ slow-moving vehicle

2. That candidate was worried about his <u>image</u>, but the other candidate didn't care what people thought.
   Ⓐ statue or representation of a person
   Ⓑ copy or likeness of a thing
   Ⓒ way the public thinks of a person
   Ⓓ equipment or baggage

3. The merchandise we bought today was far <u>superior</u> to the junk we bought last Saturday.
   Ⓐ higher in space
   Ⓑ unaffected by
   Ⓒ in charge of
   Ⓓ of higher quality

4. Margaret was very <u>vocal</u> about her opinions, but I said nothing about how I felt.
   Ⓐ spoke freely
   Ⓑ nearby
   Ⓒ hungry
   Ⓓ sung

Go on to the next page.

Context

Study Skills 6, SV 8054-5

IT'S IN THE CONTEXT (P. 2)

DIRECTIONS:

Read each sentence. Choose the best meaning for the underlined word. Fill in the answer circle in front of the correct answer.

5. The skeleton, or framework, of the building towered over the street below.
   - Ⓐ outline of a book
   - Ⓑ bones of an animal
   - Ⓒ basement entrance
   - Ⓓ supporting structure

6. The teacher was inclined to believe Robert's excuse and didn't call his parents.
   - Ⓐ sloped or slanted
   - Ⓑ superstitious
   - Ⓒ wanting or liking
   - Ⓓ behind in his work

7. The Johnsons redeemed their house loan, but the Roberts are still making monthly payments.
   - Ⓐ forgot or lost
   - Ⓑ saved or recovered
   - Ⓒ delivered from sin
   - Ⓓ paid off or back

8. The atmosphere in the room was full of anger and tension because of the agreement.
   - Ⓐ draperies and furniture
   - Ⓑ mood or feeling
   - Ⓒ air surrounding the earth
   - Ⓓ a unit of pressure

FACTS AND DETAILS

DIRECTIONS:

Read the following selection and answer the question.

An aardvark is an interesting animal. Its name comes from two Dutch words that mean "earth pig." It does resemble a pig in some ways. It spends the day curled up in the ground. At night, it rips open termite nests and uses its long, sticky tongue to gobble up a hundred thousand or more of the insects. The aardvark also eats ants.

How does the aardvark spend the day?

If you decided that the answer was that the aardvark spends the day curled up in the ground, then you were right. Often, you are asked to remember details from a story. A *detail* is a fact that supports the main idea of the selection. A detail usually answers the following questions:

Who?   What?   When?   Where?   How?

These details add interesting information to a story. Details make a story worth reading.

To Recall Specific Facts and Details:
1. READ the story carefully.
2. READ the question carefully.
3. THINK about the answer to the question.
4. REREAD the story, if necessary, to recall the detail.

Now, read the selection below and answer the question.

Henry had been angry with his dad for a week now. He wanted a dog, and his dad wouldn't let him have one. Dad had tried to explain about the apartment building rules which said, "NO DOGS!," but Henry was not listening. He wanted to blame someone, and it just turned out to be his dad. Other kids had dogs. It seemed as if everyone in his class at school had a dog – everyone except Henry.

1. Why did Henry's dad have to tell him he couldn't have a dog?

_____

Go on to the next page.

FACTS AND DETAILS (P. 2)

DIRECTIONS:

Read the selections below and answer the questions.

Among the largest of the reptiles living today are the alligators and crocodiles. Some crocodiles grow to a length of over 20 feet. Like all reptiles, alligators and crocodiles are cold-blooded and must live in warm climates. They are meat-eaters, eating fish or small animals. They cannot breathe underwater, and they lay their eggs on land. Although alligators and crocodiles are similar in looks, their heads are shaped differently, and the crocodile has a lower tooth on both sides that shows when its jaws are shut.

2. Where do alligators and crocodiles lay their eggs?

_____

3. What do alligators and crocodiles eat?

_____

4. How can you tell an alligator from a crocodile?

_____

_____

The puppy couldn't figure out who had made the mistake. He was supposed to live with his brothers and sisters and nice Mr. Gucinski at the pet store. It was great fun there! Lots of friendly people came by to visit, but, if a little fellow got tired, it was okay to curl up with the others and take a nap.

Mr. Gucinski must have been too busy to notice that these strange people had taken him. There were two big people and one little one. The little one was kind of cute, but the puppy wanted to be back at the store with his brothers and sisters. Maybe if he cried long enough, someone would take him back where he belonged.

5. Where had the puppy lived before the strange people had taken him?

_____

6. How many people were in the puppy's new family?

_____

Facts and Details

Name _____   Date _____

• •

JUST THE FACTS, PLEASE

Read the steps below.

> **Remember, To Recall Specific Facts and Details:**
> 1. READ the story carefully.
> 2. READ the question carefully.
> 3. THINK about the answer to the question.
> 4. REREAD the story, if necessary, to recall the detail.

Read the selections. Fill in the answer circle in front of the correct answers.

Asteroids travel in a path around the sun just as planets do. They are not nearly as large as a planet, but one, named Vesta, is bright enough to be seen without a telescope. The largest known asteroid is Ceres. It is less than 500 miles across. More than 1,600 asteroids have been discovered, and new ones are being found all the time.

1. What is the largest known asteroid?
Ⓐ Jupiter
Ⓑ Vesta
Ⓒ the sun
Ⓓ Ceres

When Amy had first gotten Buddy, her golden hamster, he had been only a few weeks old. He had been so small and frightened that Amy had treated him with a lot of tenderness. Buddy had learned to trust her and had grown into a fine-looking adult hamster. Now, Buddy would eat out of Amy's hand. His favorite food was crackers, but he would eat fruit, seeds, and vegetables. He was especially funny when eating a grape, because he would stuff it whole into his cheek pouch. Amy thought he looked as if he had the mumps.

2. What was Buddy's favorite food?
Ⓐ crackers
Ⓑ grapes
Ⓒ fruits
Ⓓ vegetables

Go on to the next page.

Name _____   Date _____

JUST THE FACTS, PLEASE (P. 2)

DIRECTIONS:

Read each selection. Fill in the answer circle in front of the correct answer.

Thomas Alva Edison was a remarkable man and probably the world's greatest inventor. He was known as the "Wizard of Menlo Park" because of the amazing, almost magical things he created. His most famous invention is the electric light, but he also invented the phonograph and motion pictures. Even though he made many improvements on the telegraph, he did not invent it. His sleeping habits were unusual. When working on a project in the lab, he would nap when sleepy and work upon waking, regardless of the time of day.

3. What was Thomas Edison's most famous invention?
- Ⓐ electric light
- Ⓑ telegraph
- Ⓒ phonograph
- Ⓓ motion pictures

Rodents are gnawing animals, such as rats, mice, chipmunks, beavers, and porcupines. They are mammals that live underground and above ground, in swamps and deserts, and in warm and cold areas. Their teeth never stop growing, so the constant gnawing doesn't wear them away. Most rodents eat plants, and some, like the field mouse, do a lot of damage to crops. Mice and rats are usually unwelcome visitors in our homes. The mouse is a pest, but the rat can carry dangerous diseases.

4. Why doesn't the gnawing wear away the teeth of a rodent?
- Ⓐ Rodents live underground.
- Ⓑ The teeth never stop growing.
- Ⓒ Rodents usually eat plants.
- Ⓓ Mice and rats visit our homes.

The sixth-grade class party is next Tuesday night. Only sixth-graders and their teachers can come, so no one can bring a friend in another grade, a brother, or a sister. Parents cannot come, either. There will be volleyball and basketball to play. There will be dancing, too, but a lot of children are nervous about that at first. Everyone will bring refreshments to share.

5. Who can come to the sixth-grade party?
- Ⓐ brothers and sisters
- Ⓑ sixth-graders and teachers
- Ⓒ friends and sisters
- Ⓓ parents and brothers

Facts and Details

Name_____   Date_____

• •

DETAILS, DETAILS

 **DIRECTIONS:**

Read the steps below.

> **To Recall Specific Facts and Details:**
> 1. READ the story carefully.
> 2. READ the question carefully.
> 3. THINK about the answer to the question.
> 4. REREAD the story, if necessary, to recall the detail.

Now, read each story. Fill in the answer circle in front of the correct answer.

The Sahara is the largest desert in the world. In fact, it is almost as large as the United States. It is very dry and hot in the Sahara. The highest temperature recorded was 136.4 degrees Fahrenheit, and that was in the shade! There is a little rain, and some grass can grow after the rain. Therefore, herders move their animals from place to place trying to find grass and water. The herders are called nomads and live in easily moved tents. Any permanent house has thick walls of brick that help keep the inside cool. The only place crops can be grown is in an oasis, such as the one near the Nile River. These rare green places in the desert are usually very small.

1. How do the herders find grass for their animals?
Ⓐ live in an oasis
Ⓑ move from place to place
Ⓒ build houses with thick walls
Ⓓ grow crops in an oasis

Every time my dad and Uncle Tomas get together, they have an argument. It is usually about something that happened when they were growing up together. Mom and Aunt Nora just ignore the two of them because they have never actually traded punches. They are very loud, however. The last time they were yelling so loud that the neighbors complained to our landlord. It was embarrassing. Last week, my dad had to go to the hospital because of his heart. It was strange to see Uncle Tomas sitting quietly at Dad's bedside with tears running down his face.

2. What did Dad and Uncle Tomas usually argue about?
Ⓐ something that happened growing up
Ⓑ neighbors complaining to the landlord
Ⓒ Mom and Aunt Nora ignoring them
Ⓓ my dad going to the hospital

Go on to the next page.

Facts and Details

Study Skills 6, SV 8054-5

DETAILS, DETAILS (P. 2)

DIRECTIONS:

Read each story. Fill in the answer circle in front of the correct answer.

Franklin D. Roosevelt, our 32nd president, is the only person who has held that office for more than two terms. When he was first elected, the country was in bad shape. Businesses were failing, and banks were closing their doors. He enacted some programs that gave people hope and was easily elected for a second term. By the time his second term was finished, the United States was involved in World War II. The people did not want to change presidents in the middle of the war, so Roosevelt was elected to a third and fourth term. He died before his fourth term was finished and didn't see the end of the war.

3. Why was Roosevelt elected to his second term?
Ⓐ It was the middle of the war.
Ⓑ Businesses were failing.
Ⓒ He didn't see the end of the war.
Ⓓ His programs gave people hope.

Have you ever won a contest? I hadn't until last year when I won a trip to Washington, D.C. I won the trip for writing an essay telling what it means to me to be an American. I left in June, after school was out for the summer, and stayed for two weeks in a great hotel near the Capitol. My older sister went with me because Mom had to work, so she got to meet the President, too. The only bad thing about the whole trip was that when I got back to school, they made me write an essay on what it means to me to have met the President.

4. What was the winning essay about?
Ⓐ meeting the President
Ⓑ staying near the Capitol
Ⓒ Mom having to work
Ⓓ being an American

Facts and Details

Name _____ Date _____

....

SEQUENCE

**DIRECTIONS:**

Read the following passage and think about the order in which the events occurred.

Brenda came straight home from school to practice her piano lesson. She knew she had to practice before her mother would let her go to the mall with her friends. After practicing, Brenda changed into her jeans, and then called her friends to say she was ready to go.

In what order did the events occur? Number the following events in order:

1. _____ Brenda changed into her jeans.
   _____ Brenda practiced the piano lesson.
   _____ Brenda called her friends.
   _____ Brenda came home from school.

What happened first? Brenda came home from school. (1)
What happened after she did that? Brenda practiced the piano lesson. (2)
What happened after she practiced? She changed into her jeans. (3)
What happened after she changed? She called her friends. (4)

Sometimes it is important to get the sequence, or order of events, in mind so that you can understand the story. Certain words are helpful in doing this. Words such as *first, next, then,* and *finally* can act as signals that show the order of events.

In the story above about Brenda, what had to be done before Brenda could go to the mall? Yes, Brenda had to practice. Sometimes it is necessary to put things in order according to their importance. In this case, practicing had to come before going to the mall. It was more important.

> **To Arrange Events in Order:**
> 1. READ the story carefully.
> 2. LOOK for signal words that show the order of events.
> 3. THINK about the sequence, or order of events, OR
> 4. THINK about the importance of each event.
> 5. DECIDE in what order to put the events.

Now, read the passage. Number the events in the order of importance.

Denny had to write a science report, and he needed more information from the library. His teacher said he could add a drawing if he wanted.

2. _____ Denny will get information for his report.
   _____ Denny will draw a picture for his report.

Go on to the next page.

SEQUENCE (P. 2)

DIRECTIONS:

Read each passage. Number the events in the order that they occurred.

3. They moved into the new place on February 1. The Browns had saved a long time so they could afford to buy their dream house. It wasn't a new house, so there was work to be done. First, they had to strip off the old wallpaper and prepare the walls for painting. The woodwork had to be sanded and refinished. Then, they painted the walls and cleaned every cupboard, closet, and corner. It was exciting to see the old house take on new life. On May 1, they had the project completed. It had taken three months of hard work, but it was worth every minute of it.

_____ finishing the project on May 1
_____ painting the walls
_____ moving into the new place
_____ stripping off old wallpaper
_____ saving money for the house

4. The children in the neighborhood got together last Saturday to build a clubhouse. They collected building materials from home and brought them to the empty lot. First, they looked for a flat spot away from the street. Then, they began erecting the walls. After the walls were in place, the roof was constructed. Last of all, the whole thing was painted orange. It was the only color paint anybody's parents would give them. It looked bright, but terrific! It would never be a secret clubhouse, but it was all theirs.

_____ constructed the roof
_____ brought materials from home
_____ painted the clubhouse orange
_____ looked for a flat place
_____ erected the walls

Read the passage. Number the items in the order of their importance to the camping trip.

5. Jay had to remember the food for the camping trip. He also wanted to take the camera. If he had time today, he would call his friend Jimmy about going to the movies next Saturday.

_____ call Jimmy
_____ take food
_____ take the camera

Name_____   Date_____

PUTTING IT IN ORDER

 **DIRECTIONS:**

Read the steps below.

> **Remember, To Arrange Events in Order:**
> 1. READ the story carefully.
> 2. LOOK for the signal words that show the order of events.
> 3. THINK about the sequence, or order of events, OR
> 4. THINK about the importance of each event.
> 5. DECIDE in what order to put the events.

Now, read each passage and fill in the answer circle in front of the choice that best answers the question.

Stephanie wanted a special dress for the program at school next month. Her mom was short of money this month, and she told Stephanie she'd have to earn the money herself. First, she decided what jobs she could do in the hours after school and on weekends. Baby-sitting and dog-walking would be good possibilities. Then, she put up notices with her phone number at the neighborhood stores. After going to the stores, Stephanie put notices in mailboxes near her house. She even asked her mom to tell people at work that she was available.

1. What did Stephanie do after going to the stores?
- Ⓐ Stephanie asked Mom for the money.
- Ⓑ Mom said she was short of money.
- Ⓒ Stephanie decided on the jobs.
- Ⓓ Stephanie put notices in mailboxes.

2. What happened last?
- Ⓐ Stephanie put notices in mailboxes.
- Ⓑ Stephanie put notices in stores.
- Ⓒ Stephanie asked Mom to tell people.
- Ⓓ Mom was short of money and couldn't help.

These are some things people need to live a healthy, happy life: food, friends, oxygen, shelter, entertainment, and water.

3. Which one of these things would be needed before the others?
- Ⓐ food   Ⓑ oxygen
- Ⓒ water   Ⓓ shelter

Go on to the next page.

Sequence

PUTTING IT IN ORDER (P. 2)

DIRECTIONS:

Read each passage. Fill in the answer circle in front of the choice that best answers the question.

Washing the car was Tony's Saturday job. He had a routine worked out so everything was done exactly right. First, he made sure the windows were tightly closed. He'd made the mistake of leaving one open before. What a mess! Then, he sprayed the car to wet it. Next, he carefully washed each part of the car and rinsed frequently so the soap wouldn't dry. After letting the car air-dry a few minutes, Tony dried it with a soft towel. If the inside needed vacuuming, he saved it for last. Tony felt proud of the way the car looked when he finished.

4. What did Tony do just before he dried the car with a soft towel?
- Ⓐ He let the car air-dry for a few minutes.
- Ⓑ He washed and rinsed each part of the car.
- Ⓒ He felt proud of the way the car looked.
- Ⓓ He sprayed the car to wet it.

5. What did Tony do first?
- Ⓐ He sprayed the car to wet it.
- Ⓑ He vacuumed the inside of the car.
- Ⓒ He left a window open on the car.
- Ⓓ He made sure the windows were closed.

These are some people who work for our government: the Secretary of State, the mail carrier, an FBI agent, the President, and the Education Secretary.

6. Who is the most important to the government of the United States?
- Ⓐ the mail carrier
- Ⓑ the Secretary of State
- Ⓒ an FBI agent
- Ⓓ the President

• •

BEFORE AND AFTER

 **DIRECTIONS:**

Read the steps below.

> **To Arrange Events in Order:**
> 1. READ the story carefully.
> 2. LOOK for signal words that show the order of events.
> 3. THINK about the sequence, or order of events.
> 4. DECIDE in what order events occurred.

Now, read each story. Fill in the answer circle in front of the correct answer.

Sedimentary rocks are formed by the building up of layers of material on the bottom of lakes and oceans. First, sand, gravel, and mud are washed into the lake or ocean from the land. At the same time, the bodies of dead animals fall to the floor of the lakes and oceans. These materials form thick layers on the bottom. The layers then stick together and eventually become sedimentary rock.

1. Right before the materials become rock, they _____.

Ⓐ are washed into the lake

Ⓑ stick together

Ⓒ form thick layers

Ⓓ become sedimentary rock

The students in room 206 started their own bank and money system. First, they built a bank out of donated lumber. They had money printed on bright green paper. After that, the teacher decided what jobs needed to be done in the room and then interviewed and hired someone for each job. When all of these preparations were done, the children began earning money by doing their jobs. At the end of the school year, everyone agreed that the bank and the money system had been successes.

2. Right before they printed the money, the children _____.

Ⓐ built a bank out of lumber

Ⓑ began earning money

Ⓒ interviewed for a job

Ⓓ agreed it was a success

Go on to the next page.

BEFORE AND AFTER (P. 2)

DIRECTIONS:

Read each story. Fill in the answer circle in front of the correct answer.

In the spring, robins fly north after having spent the winter in a warmer climate. They select a place for a nest. It may be quite near a house because robins don't seem to mind being in full view of humans. They then collect sticks, leaves, and grass to build a strong nest. After the nest is completed, the female robin lays from three to five blue eggs. When the eggs hatch, the baby robins keep their parents busy feeding them worms and insects. They have feathers in ten days, but don't have the parents' bright orange breast until later.

3. After the eggs hatch, the robins _____.
   Ⓐ feed the hungry babies
   Ⓑ fly north in the spring
   Ⓒ collect sticks, leaves, and grass
   Ⓓ select a place for a nest

Jeri has the same routine every night when she does homework for school. First, she makes sure her parents will keep her little brother busy and out of her room. Then, she takes her books upstairs to her room. There, she puts everything on her desk and checks to be sure she has paper and pencil. After working for about an hour, Jeri goes downstairs for a snack and a drink. Before going back to work, Jeri spends a few minutes playing with her cat. After finishing her homework, Jeri usually watches television or calls a friend.

4. Before going down for a snack, Jeri _____.
   Ⓐ watches television
   Ⓑ takes her books upstairs
   Ⓒ makes sure she has paper
   Ⓓ works for about an hour

5. Just after her snack, Jeri _____.
   Ⓐ watches television
   Ⓑ plays with her cat
   Ⓒ calls a friend
   Ⓓ puts everything on her desk

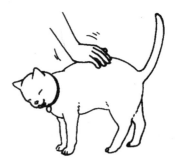

Sequence

Name _____   Date _____

FIRST, NEXT, AND LAST

 **DIRECTIONS:**

Read each story. Fill in the answer circle in front of the correct answer.

Before there were any man-made fibers, silk was thought to be the most beautiful cloth. Cotton and linen were strong and washable, but silk was too expensive to be worn by everybody. In 1891, Count Chardonnet, a French scientist, invented a fiber by changing cotton into a liquid and then hardening it into threads. He called it artificial silk. Thirty-five years later, it was brought to the United States and was called rayon. Rayon can be dyed beautiful colors and will last a long time. Today it is very popular. A billion pounds of it are used every year.

1. Before rayon is hardened into threads, it is _____.
- Ⓐ dyed beautiful colors
- Ⓑ strong and washable
- Ⓒ brought to the United States
- Ⓓ changed from cotton into a liquid

Jasmine wakes up in the morning and stretches. Then her blue eyes open wide as she looks to see if Maggie is awake. Maggie is a little girl, and little girls have to go to school. Jasmine, on the other hand, is fortunate. She's a lovely Siamese cat who gets to do anything she wants all day long. Jasmine walks to the window and checks the yard before going down to breakfast. After breakfast, Jasmine finds the warmest, sunniest spot in the house for her morning bath. Jasmine calmly decides how her day will begin, knowing that her life is purr-fect!

2. First of all this morning, Jasmine _____.
- Ⓐ wakes up and stretches
- Ⓑ finds the warmest spot
- Ⓒ looks at Maggie
- Ⓓ walks to the window

3. Before going down to breakfast, Jasmine _____.
- Ⓐ finds a sunny spot
- Ⓑ has her bath
- Ⓒ checks the yard
- Ⓓ walks and stretches

Go on to the next page.

Sequence

Study Skills 6, SV 8054-5

FIRST, NEXT, AND LAST (P. 2)

DIRECTIONS:

Read each story. Fill in the answer circle in front of the correct answer.

Many millions of people in Asia follow the teachings of Buddha. Buddha was born in India about 2,500 years ago. His father was a rajah, or king, and Buddha lived a happy, protected childhood in the royal palace. Then, he began leaving the palace and saw the suffering of the people. At the age of 29, he decided to go to the mountains and to think about the reason for all of the misery in the world. After a few years, he returned and found peace among the people. For the next 45 years, Buddha walked the land teaching peace and acceptance. All of the thousands of temples throughout Asia contain statues of the beloved Buddha.

4. After Buddha saw the suffering of the people, he _____.
Ⓐ lived a protected childhood
Ⓑ found peace among the people
Ⓒ began leaving the palace
Ⓓ decided to go to the mountains

Morris began preparing the meal for his dad's birthday by making a salad. Then he spilled it on the floor. When he set the table, he broke two glasses and a plate. Next, he burned the cake and forgot to add cheese to the macaroni and cheese casserole. The worst was when he noticed the puddle of ice cream melted all over the counter. Morris closed the kitchen door and went to the phone. He had decided birthday candles would look great on a nice, big pizza!

5. Before burning the cake, Morris _____.
Ⓐ forgot to add cheese
Ⓑ noticed the puddle
Ⓒ broke two glasses and a plate
Ⓓ called out for pizza

6. After Morris noticed the puddle of ice cream, he _____.
Ⓐ went to the phone
Ⓑ set the table
Ⓒ made a salad
Ⓓ burned the cake

Name_____   Date_____

PERSUASIVE DEVICES

How does a writer persuade the reader to buy a product, vote for a candidate, or change his or her mind?

These are five persuasive techniques. Write an example of your own after each one.

1. Bandwagon
The writer tries to convince you to do something because others are.
Example: Buy Sudsy Soap! It's the soap of the smartest shoppers.

_____

2. Glad words/sad words
The writer makes the subject seem better or worse than it really is by carefully choosing words.
Example: Sudsy Soap makes your skin deliciously smooth and soft.

_____

3. Glittering generalities
The writer uses phrases that make a general statement with no details to support it.
Example: Sudsy Soap is the best in the world!

_____

4. Plain folks
The writer wants you to think that the person speaking is a real person just like you.
Example: Candidate Sincere knows about your problems. She and her family live right here in Monroe County.

_____

_____

5. Snob appeal/testimonial
The writer wants you to think that only the best people know the value of this product. Sometimes a famous person is paid to give a testimony for the product.
Example: Billy Baseball says, "I know how Sudsy Soap works. I use it after a tough game. You should try it, too."

_____

_____

To Recognize Persuasive Devices:

1. READ or LISTEN carefully to the writer's statement.

2. THINK about the meaning of the statement.

3. DECIDE whether or not a persuasive technique is being used.

Name _____ Date _____

THE POWER OF PERSUASION

DIRECTIONS:

Read the steps below.

> **To Recognize Persuasive Devices:**
> 1. READ or LISTEN carefully to the writer's statement.
> 2. THINK about the meaning of the statement.
> 3. DECIDE whether or not a persuasive technique is being used.

Read these statements. Fill in the answer circle in front of the choice that best answers the question.

1. Henrietta Homemaker has a family just like yours, and she works hard just like you. She uses Kwik Kleaner.

   Which persuasive technique was used?
   Ⓐ glad words/sad words
   Ⓑ glittering generalities
   Ⓒ plain folks
   Ⓓ no persuasive technique

2. You will have the most beautiful hair in the world if you use Wonderful Tress Shampoo.

   Which persuasive technique was used?
   Ⓐ glad words/sad words
   Ⓑ glittering generalities
   Ⓒ plain folks
   Ⓓ no persuasive technique

3. Steve Superstar says, "I use Shiny Car Wax on my Ferrari. You'll like it, too."

   Which persuasive technique was used?
   Ⓐ glad words/sad words
   Ⓑ glittering generalities
   Ⓒ snob appeal/testimonial
   Ⓓ plain folks

Go on to the next page.

Name_____   Date_____

THE POWER OF PERSUASION (P. 2)

DIRECTIONS:

Read these statements. Fill in the answer circle in front of the choice that best answers the question.

4. Everyone else is using Miracle Mask Makeup. Why aren't you?

   Which persuasive technique was used?
   - Ⓐ glad words/sad words
   - Ⓑ plain folks
   - Ⓒ bandwagon
   - Ⓓ no persuasive technique

5. For the comfort and softness you deserve, buy Fluffy Tissues. You feel only a gentle caress as they touch your delicate skin.

   Which persuasive technique was used?
   - Ⓐ glad words/sad words
   - Ⓑ plain folks
   - Ⓒ glittering generalities
   - Ⓓ no persuasive technique

6. Try Almond and Chocolate Breakfast Cereal. You might like it.

   Which persuasive technique was used?
   - Ⓐ glad words/sad words
   - Ⓑ plain folks
   - Ⓒ snob appeal/testimonial
   - Ⓓ no persuasive device

7. If you want to be one of the Beautiful People, wear Posh Perfume.

   Which persuasive technique was used?
   - Ⓐ glad words/sad words
   - Ⓑ plain folks
   - Ⓒ glittering generalities
   - Ⓓ snob appeal/testimonial

Persuasive Devices
Study Skills 6, SV 8054-5

SUMMARY

 **DIRECTIONS:**

Read this story and think about how you would tell the main idea and important events in one or two sentences.

Nancy was alone in the house when she heard the sound of breaking glass outside. She got a flashlight and her dog and then went to investigate. A window was broken in the empty house next door.

You can retell, or summarize, this story if you decide what the most important parts of the story are. In this case, you would probably say something like this:

Nancy went outside to investigate a sound and found a broken window next door.

When you tell a shortened form of a story, you are making a summary. A *summary* is a short account of the main idea and important points in an article. There are some parts of the story or article that will be left out of your summary. That is because they are less important than the parts you include. They may make the story interesting, but you can tell the story without them.

> **To Summarize a Story:**
> 1. READ the story carefully.
> 2. THINK about its main idea and important points.
> 3. INCLUDE only those ideas in your summary.

Now, read these selections and write a summary of each.

1. It was a rainy Saturday, and the girls were stuck inside. There was nothing on television, and neither one of them wanted to play the usual rainy-day games. Then, Marla had a brainstorm! They could write a play and perform it for all the family tomorrow after dinner.

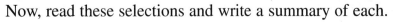

_____

_____

2. Phillipe wished that his birthday would hurry up and get here. His papa had said that when Phillipe was 12, he could help in the shop. Papa was a wonderful carpenter, and Phillipe wanted to learn to use his hands with the same skill. To work with the dark, beautiful woods was his greatest dream.

_____

_____

Name_____   Date_____

SUMMING IT UP

Read the steps below.

> **To Summarize a Story:**
> 1. READ the story carefully.
> 2. THINK about its main idea and important points.
> 3. INCLUDE only those ideas in your summary.

Now, read these selections. Fill in the answer circle in front of the choice that best answers the question.

Carol loved the feeling of skiing down a long, smooth slope. The movements of her body were graceful, and she enjoyed the exercise. The cool, crisp air made her feel glad to be alive. This was her favorite place in the whole world.

1. Which of these statements is the best summary?
Ⓐ Carol loves snow.
Ⓑ Skiing is Carol's favorite activity.
Ⓒ Carol wants to be a championship skier.
Ⓓ Long, smooth slopes are important to skiing.

Sally and Sharon got to the theater late and missed the beginning of the movie. As they climbed over people to find a seat, Sharon spilled popcorn on a lady's head. During the movie, a man behind them insisted on making very loud comments about the actors. To make things worse, the movie was really bad. They wished they'd stayed home and watched television.

2. Which of these statements is the best summary?
Ⓐ Television is always better than going to the movies.
Ⓑ Sally and Sharon had an awful time at the movies.
Ⓒ People shouldn't eat popcorn or talk during movies.
Ⓓ Arriving late to any social occasion is impolite.

Go on to the next page.

Name _____ Date _____

....

SUMMING IT UP (P. 2)

DIRECTIONS:

Read the selections. Fill in the answer circle in front of the choice that best answers the question.

Freddie had an aquarium in his room. He had a dish containing two turtles, Pokey and Flash. His hamster, Caesar, had a fancy cage on the dresser. The tadpoles he had caught in the pond were swimming in the big, glass pickle jar by the window. His tarantula, Harry, lived in a desert-like terrarium by his bed. Freddie didn't have brothers and sisters, but he had lots of animal friends.

3. Which of these statements is the best summary?
Ⓐ Tarantulas live in a desert environment.
Ⓑ Freddie was an only child and very lonely.
Ⓒ Freddie had many animals in his room.
Ⓓ Hamsters and turtles make good pets.

The spider had constructed her web using her inborn talent. The morning dewdrops shone like diamonds on it, but she didn't feel pride. She was a hunter, and a patient one. Perhaps she would catch something in her trap today; perhaps not. She could go for days without food, but when she did catch her prey, she would quickly paralyze it with her poison and eat.

4. Which of these statements is the best summary?
Ⓐ Spiders construct webs with pride.
Ⓑ Spiders can go without water for days.
Ⓒ The morning dew makes webs beautiful.
Ⓓ Spiders build webs to trap their food.

It was the year 2025. People had invented machines to do most of the work. No one had a job. It was considered old-fashioned to work. There was all the time in the world to read, think, and play. Sometimes when people got really tired of always playing, they would take a vacation to a place where they could pay to work on a job. They really looked forward to those vacations from play. It was very tiring to play all the time.

5. Which of these statements is the best summary?
Ⓐ In the future, people will still work long hours.
Ⓑ People will someday invent a machine that will think.
Ⓒ Machines will soon take over and rule the world.
Ⓓ Machines allowed the people to play all the time.

Summary

CONCLUSIONS

 **DIRECTIONS:**

Read the following story and think about its meaning.

Dana was sitting by herself at the side of the stage. She held her violin as she listened to the boy performing on stage. She nervously straightened the collar of her white blouse and glanced at the judges sitting in the front row.

What is happening in this story? It sounds like Dana is getting ready to play her violin for the judges. She is also nervous about performing. When we add up the facts to form an opinion, we are drawing conclusions. To draw a conclusion means to form an opinion based on facts and experience.

Sometimes, your conclusion may not be correct, but you can always change your opinion when you get more facts.

> **To Draw Conclusions:**
> 1. READ the story carefully.
> 2. THINK about how the facts add up.
> 3. FORM an opinion about what is happening, based on the facts and your experience.

Read the following stories and draw a conclusion for each.

1. Dana walked from the stage smiling. The judges shook her hand and handed her an award.

_____

2. Mike's parents drove up to the house. They saw a broken window and Mike sitting on the porch with his head down. He had a baseball bat in his hand.

_____

3. The swimmers got out of the pool after the race and immediately wrapped themselves in towels. They shivered as the wind hit their wet bodies.

_____

4. Mrs. Ward walked slowly out to her mailbox. Her body was bent with age, and each step seemed filled with careful effort. As she pulled the bright blue envelope from her mailbox, her face broke into a smile filled with love and appreciation.

_____

Go on to the next page.

CONCLUSIONS (P. 2)

DIRECTIONS:

Read the following stories and draw a conclusion for each.

5. The grass was turning green, and the bare branches of the trees were beginning to bud.

_____

6. Billy held his stomach and groaned with pain. An empty pie pan lay on the kitchen table.

_____

7. Tracey sat in the back of the classroom and squinted as she tried to read the chalkboard.

_____

8. The Siamese cat sat by the empty birdcage. There were a few feathers scattered around the room.

_____

9. When Mom woke up this morning, she realized the electricity was off. The electric clock still said 4:30 A.M.

_____

10. Ms. Rogers walked into the noisy classroom and calmly wrote a note about recess on the chalkboard. The children groaned as they read what it said.

_____

11. Jennifer sat outside in the grass. The sun felt warm on her soft fur. She licked her paw and rubbed her ear. She padded over and dug her claws into her favorite tree.

_____

12. When you walk into Jim's back door, you see an exercise bike and a bench press for lifting weights. There is also a pair of well-worn running shoes by the back door.

_____

WHAT IS MOST LIKELY?

 **DIRECTIONS:**

Read the steps below.

> **Remember, To Draw Conclusions:**
> 1. READ the story carefully.
> 2. THINK about how the facts add up.
> 3. FORM an opinion about what is happening, based on the facts and your experience.

Read these stories. Fill in the answer circle in front of the choice that best completes each sentence.

It was the fall of the year. The children were out of school for a few days and could be heard playing outside. The smell of turkey and dressing filled the house. Relatives had gathered for this special day.

1. It is most likely _____.
   Ⓐ Mother's Day
   Ⓑ Valentine's Day
   Ⓒ Memorial Day
   Ⓓ Thanksgiving Day

The car was loaded with luggage. We had left a note with the neighbor about feeding the dog each day for the next two weeks. We had talked to the paper girl about not leaving the paper. It was time to go!

2. It is most likely _____.
   Ⓐ moving day
   Ⓑ vacation time
   Ⓒ a garage sale
   Ⓓ time for a picnic

Vanessa came in from school with a huge pile of books. After getting a quick snack, she settled down to work.

3. She most likely is _____.
   Ⓐ to be in a school play next month
   Ⓑ going to a party tonight
   Ⓒ busy with a lot of homework
   Ⓓ ready for summer vacation

Go on to the next page.

Conclusions

• •

WHAT IS MOST LIKELY? (P. 2)

DIRECTIONS:

Read these stories. Fill in the answer circle in front of the choice that best completes each sentence.

Principal Jeffries glared at the girls again. She paced around the office. Occasionally, she asked one of them a question. They answered in low voices and kept their heads down the rest of the time. She reread the note from the playground supervisor and shook her head.

4. Principal Jeffries is most likely _____.
- Ⓐ preparing to congratulate the girls for doing a fine job
- Ⓑ going to discipline the girls for misbehaving outside
- Ⓒ thinking about what she will do at home after school
- Ⓓ deciding whether the school will have a baseball team

The dog lies in the shade. He is panting heavily. He frequently walks to his empty water dish and licks the bottom.

5. It is most likely _____.
- Ⓐ the middle of winter
- Ⓑ storming outside
- Ⓒ a pet store sale
- Ⓓ very hot and dry

The Braddocks went out into the front yard and proudly removed the "FOR SALE" sign from the lawn. They began taking boxes of belongings from the car and carrying them into the house.

6. It is most likely that the Braddocks _____.
- Ⓐ are moving out of the house
- Ⓑ are professional movers
- Ⓒ would like to buy a house
- Ⓓ are moving into the house

The cat scratched to come inside. After we let him in, he shook the water from his fur.

7. It is most likely _____.
- Ⓐ time for dinner
- Ⓑ raining outside
- Ⓒ really cold
- Ⓓ hot and dry

Conclusions

WHAT CAN YOU CONCLUDE?

DIRECTIONS:

Read the steps below.

Remember, To Draw Conclusions:
1. **READ the story carefully.**
2. **THINK about how the facts add up.**
3. **FORM an opinion about what is happening, based on the facts and your experience.**

Now, read each story. Fill in the answer circle in front of the correct answer.

Louis Braille invented a simple written language for the blind. Being blind himself, he understood how necessary reading is to a blind person. Now, books, newspapers, and magazines are printed in Braille.

1. Which of the following can be concluded from the passage?
- Ⓐ Louis Braille was also deaf and couldn't speak.
- Ⓑ Braille uses raised dots to make letters.
- Ⓒ The blind can now read books and magazines.
- Ⓓ Louis Braille also invented a Braille typewriter.

It was 11:45 Friday when the bell rang, and the children walked out the door. The teacher said, "Have a nice, long weekend. See you on Monday!"

2. Which of the following can be concluded from the passage?
- Ⓐ School is out for summer vacation.
- Ⓑ There has been a fire at the school.
- Ⓒ The children are getting the afternoon off.
- Ⓓ The teacher is quitting and won't be back.

Daniel Boone was born in a wilderness area in Pennsylvania. His family later moved to a desolate area in North Carolina. After cutting the Wilderness Road into Kentucky, Boone moved his wife and his daughter into the area. Later in life, Boone moved still farther west, where he could explore the Rockies.

3. Which of the following can be concluded from the passage?
- Ⓐ Daniel Boone liked living in settled areas.
- Ⓑ Daniel Boone fought in the French and Indian War.
- Ⓒ Daniel Boone learned many of the Indian ways.
- Ⓓ Boone was always moving west into uncharted areas.

Go on to the next page.

Name _____   Date _____

DIRECTIONS:

Read each story. Fill in the answer circle in front of the correct answer.

Mrs. Carter had a worried look on her face as she glanced at the clock. She shouted out the door once again for her son. Then, she telephoned the neighbors to ask if they had seen him. It was getting dark outside, and the street looked deserted.

4. Which of the following can be concluded from the passage?
  Ⓐ The Carter family is going to a movie tonight.
  Ⓑ Mrs. Carter's son is late getting home tonight.
  Ⓒ Her son has probably had trouble with his paper route.
  Ⓓ The neighbors said that he was on his way home.

Quarrying for rock involves cutting and drilling large enough blocks of rock to use in building. Quarries in Egypt have been providing building rock for 4,500 years. Across the Nile from where the limestone pyramids stand are even older quarries.

5. Which of the following can be concluded from the passage?
  Ⓐ In early quarries, a big problem was moving the rock.
  Ⓑ Crushed rock is very important to road building.
  Ⓒ The pyramids are located in Giza near the Nile River.
  Ⓓ Quarrying for building rock is not a new occupation.

Marty and Stan sat in class glaring at each other. The teacher had to ask them to pay attention. When recess came, they stayed on opposite ends of the playground, even though they usually played together.

6. Which of the following can be concluded from the passage?
  Ⓐ Marty and Stan had a fist fight during the last recess.
  Ⓑ Stan didn't invite Marty to his birthday party.
  Ⓒ Stan and Marty are usually friends, but are angry today.
  Ⓓ Marty called Stan a cheater the last time they played.

Conclusions

Study Skills Grade 6
Answer Key

• •

Assessment: pp. 6-8
1. first name underlined; date written under name
2. 1995 and 1997
3. 2 hours, 30 minutes
4. C
5. B
6. A
7. I was at home sick, while my friends were at school making surprise get-well notes for me.
8. C
9. A
10. B
11. opinion
12. circle *she loaned hers to me;* underline *Kay didn't have a pencil*
13. The Davis family will go back to the cottage.
14. Several people in my family are teachers.
15. A. invalid opinion
    B. valid opinion
    C. true statement
    D. valid opinion
16. B
17. C
18. the electric light
19. 3, 1, 2
20. A
21. B

P. 9
1. a circle with the word *blue* inside; a box around the circle; first name in cursive under the box
2. two dots connected with a straight line; *HELLO* printed above the line

P. 10
1. A
2. C
3. B
4. C

Pp. 11-12
1. Jean
2. notice
3. kneel
4. shine
5. pit
6. first
7. roll
8. she
9. pen
10. first
11. rack
12. car
13. second
14. Fay
15. cut
16. day

Pp. 13-14
1. Greek
2. gramma
3. Latin
4. nodus
5. a knot
6. Latin
7. carrus
8. chariot
9. American Indian

Pp. 15-16
1. reading
2. parents, teachers, or librarians
3. D
4. D
5. C
6. B

Pp. 17-18
1. A
2. B
3. D
4. B
5. D
6. A
7. B

Pp. 19-20
1. subject
2. thesaurus
3. author
4. title
5. subject
6. encyclopedia
7. dictionary
8. telephone directory
9. newspaper
10. almanac

Pp. 21-22
1. C
2. A
3. C
4. A
5. D
6. B
7. B
8. A
9. D
10. D

Pp. 23-24
1. footnote
2. appendix
3. appendix
4. footnote
5. footnote
6. appendix
7. C
8. B
9. A
10. C
11. B

Pp. 25-26
1. B
2. C

3. A
4. D
5. A
6. B
7. D
8. D

Pp. 27-28
Answers will vary.
1. Sal was angry and determined to stand up to Lenny.
2. She is afraid of her mother's friend.
3. D
4. C
5. A
6. D

P. 29
1. He (she) wore his (her) new shoes to school yesterday.
2. He (she) drove the truck by him(her)self until his (her) father made him (her) stop.

P. 30
1. C
2. A
3. C
4. B
5. B

P. 31
1. 30th of May, 1922
2. Washington, D.C.
3. last fall
4. small town

P. 32
1. B
2. C
3. D
4. D

P. 33
historical fiction; answers may vary: Possible words underlined: The *Mayflower,* voyage, her mother had helped with the birth of a baby; The *Mayflower* was a real part of history, and the story is possible.

P. 34
1 A
2. B
3. C
4. A

P. 35
Answers will vary.
1. The bushes lay close to the ground in our backyard.
2. The sailboat moved smoothly past us.

3. Winter snow fell to the ground.
4. The tulip bloom swayed in the breeze.
5. The rock lay in the sun by the stream.

P. 36
1. B
2. A
3. A
4. B
5. B
6. A
7. B

Pp. 37-38
1. C
2. B
3. D
4. A

Pp. 39-40
1. A
2. D
3. A
4. D
5. B

Pp. 41-42
circle *Because her shoes were too tight;* underline *her feet hurt*
1. underline *I like to go to the circus;* circle *because of the clowns*
2. circle *Since you gave me a dollar;* underline *I can buy the candy*
3. circle *It was hot outside;* underline *therefore, Joe wore his shorts*
4. circle *Jill forgot to shut the door;* underline *so the dog got out*
5. circle *Since Sarah has a computer;* underline *we worked at her house*
6. underline *Ronnie liked the cupcakes;* circle *because they were chocolate*
7. underline *Kay didn't have a pencil;* circle *since she loaned hers to me*
8. circle *Because Mom called us for supper;* underline *we couldn't play anymore*
9. underline *Mom lit the candles;* circle *because the electricity was out*
10. circle *The invention is mine;* underline *therefore, he can't take the credit*

Answers will vary.
11. I didn't remember your birthday because I was really busy.
12. I missed the school bus because my mother forgot to wake me up.

Pp. 43-44
1. A
2. B
3. A
4. A
5. B
6. D

Pp. 45-46
1. C
2. D
3. D
4. C
5. C
6. A

Pp. 47-48
1. B
2. D
3. C
4. A
5. B
6. D

Pp. 49-50
1. Patricia will ask Tara's dad to take her to school.
2. Patricia will walk to school.
3. Jake will get a drink at the fountain.
4. Jake will get in the car and drink the juice.
5. Tina will sit at the desk by the teacher.
6. The Davis family will go back to the cottage.
7. They will roast hot dogs and marshmallows in the fireplace in the cottage.

Pp. 51-52
1. A
2. B
3. C
4. B
5. D
6. C

P. 53
1. Some birds are brightly colored.
2. Several people in my family are teachers.
3. Most of our class does not wear glasses.

Pp. 54-55
1. B
2. C
3. C
4. A
5. A
6. B
7. C
P. 56
1. B
2. A
Pp. 57-58
1. B
2. B
3. A
4. C
5. A
6. A
7. C
8. B
9. A
10. C
11. B
Pp. 59-60
1. C
2. The story tells about the hunting skills of a mongoose.
3. D
4. The story tells about Peter's talent for fixing things.
5. A
6. The story tells of how he was not paid for his work and had no friends or home.
Pp. 61-62
1. D
2. B
3. B
4. C
5. A
Pp. 63-64
1. D
2. D
3. B
4. C
5. C
6. A
Pp. 65-66
1. need
2. break
3. look like
4. hot and moist
5. B
6. C
7. B
Pp. 67-68
1. B
2. C
3. D
4. A

5. D
6. C
7. D
8. B
Pp. 69-70
1. The rules for the apartment building said, "No dogs!"
2. They lay their eggs on land.
3. Alligators and crocodiles eat fish or small animals.
4. Their heads are shaped differently, and the crocodile has a lower tooth that shows when its jaws are shut.
5. The puppy lived in a pet store.
6. There were three people in the puppy's new family.
Pp. 71-72
1. D
2. A
3. A
4. B
5. B
Pp. 73-74
1. B
2. A
3. D
4. D
Pp. 75-76
1. 3, 2, 4, 1
2. 1, 2
3. 5, 4, 2, 3, 1
4. 4, 1, 5, 2, 3
5. 3, 1, 2
Pp. 77-78
1. D
2. C
3. B
4. A
5. D
6. D
Pp. 79-80
1. B
2. A
3. A
4. D
5. B
Pp. 81-82
1. D
2. A
3. C
4. D
5. C
6. A
P. 83
Answers will vary but should follow the rule of the persuasive technique.

Pp. 84-85
1. C
2. B
3. C
4. C
5. A
6. D
7. D
P. 86
Answers will vary.
1. One rainy day, Marla got the idea to write a play to perform for the family.
2. Phillipe wanted to work in the carpenter shop with his dad.
Pp. 87-88
1. B
2. B
3. C
4. D
5. D
Pp. 89-90
1. Dana won an award for playing the violin.
2. Mike has broken the window.
3. The weather is cool for the swim meet.
4. Mrs. Ward got a card from a loved one.
5. It is spring.
6. Billy ate the whole pie.
7. Tracey needed glasses.
8. The cat ate the bird.
9. The electricity went off at 4:30 A.M.
10. The children have lost their recess.
11. Jennifer is a cat.
12. Jim likes to exercise.
Pp. 91-92
1. D
2. B
3. C
4. B
5. D
6. D
7. B
Pp. 93-94
1. C
2. C
3. D
4. B
5. D
6. C